"In *Not All Roads Lead to Heaven,* Dr. Jeffress has given the body of Christ a great tool. The exclusivity of the Christian gospel is not just a theological issue to be debated, it is the heart and soul of the gospel."

Dr. David Jeremiah, senior pastor, Shadow Mountain
Community Church; founder and president,
Turning Point Ministries

"Jesus said He was the exclusive means to know God His Father and to come to His Father for salvation and a home in heaven. Either Jesus was right or He wasn't. I believe He was right. And my friend Robert Jeffress believes He was right. Whether you do or don't, this book deserves a serious read. I believe it asks and answers one of the most critical questions of our time—the one that actually determines a person's eternal destiny."

Dr. Mark L. Bailey, president and senior professor
of Bible exposition, Dallas Theological Seminary

"These are desperate times not just because evil runs rampant but because we as Christians have lost the clarity of the gospel. Scripture tells us that while we were *dead* in our sins, Christ died *for* us. We weren't in need of a slight upgrade, a makeover, or a temporary loan to get us on our feet again. *We were destined for hell.* Totally incapable of saving ourselves. And in that place of our utter and desperate need—while our selfishness, sinfulness, and pride were in full swing—Christ died *for us.* That's amazingly good news! So why have we watered down and changed our message to a world so desperately in need? It's time for a reset. I'm grateful you found this book! In *Not All Roads Lead to Heaven,* Dr. Jeffress masterfully addresses the common arguments against biblical Christianity and equips us to engage with those who disagree with Christ's claims about Himself. Dr. Jeffress aims to help us to more clearly articulate the good news that Jesus came to save sinners because He loves them. Read this book. It's a must-read for the day in which we live."

Susie Larson, talk radio host, national speaker, and author

"What a shock it will be someday for many people who will arrive in eternity only to discover all roads don't lead to heaven. This book will provide solid answers as to why this is so. You will learn why Jesus alone has the qualifications to be the Savior."

Dr. Erwin W. Lutzer, senior pastor,
the Moody Church, Chicago

"*Not All Roads Lead to Heaven* is the most important book Dr. Robert Jeffress has penned. Scintillating, faithful to the Bible, and controversial among non-evangelicals, Jeffress veers neither to the right nor to the left but faithfully elucidates the words and intentions of Jesus. Do not bypass this book!"

Paige Patterson, president, Southwestern Baptist
Theological Seminary

"Every rational, logical thinker needs the content of this book, because in the end eternity is too long to be wrong."

June Hunt, founder, CSO Hope for the Heart

"Not only is Robert Jeffress as straight as an arrow theologically but he, like the apostles of old, is also moved with a passionate longing to see every person on the planet come to personal faith in Jesus Christ. The Lord's question in Matthew 16:15 has become the question of our time—'Who do you say that I am?' Is He, in fact, 'the way, the truth and the life,' and do we really believe that 'no one comes to the Father unless they come through Him'? In this volume Dr. Jeffress hits the bull's-eye on this important subject."

O. S. Hawkins, president/CEO,
GuideStone Financial Resources

"*Not All Roads Lead to Heaven* will help you remember the greatest answers for believing and defending the true gospel story. I wholeheartedly recommend it to all Christians, pastors, and Bible teachers, for it will warm your heart and mind with 'the reason for the hope that is in us.'"

Dr. Tim LaHaye, pastor, author, and Christian educator

NOT
ALL ROADS
LEAD
to HEAVEN

NOT
ALL ROADS
LEAD
to HEAVEN

Sharing an Exclusive Jesus
in an Inclusive World

Dr. Robert Jeffress

BakerBooks
a division of Baker Publishing Group
Grand Rapids, Michigan

Published by Baker Books
a division of Baker Publishing Group
P.O. Box 6287, Grand Rapids, MI 49516-6287
www.bakerbooks.com

Printed in the United States of America

Library of Congress Cataloging-in-Publication Data
Jeffress, Robert, 1955– author.
    Not all roads lead to heaven : sharing an exclusive Jesus in an inclusive world / Dr. Robert Jeffress.
        pages cm
    Includes bibliographical references.
    ISBN 978-0-8010-1875-6 (cloth)
    ISBN 978-0-8010-1916-6 (ITPE)
    1. Salvation—Christianity. 2. Jesus Christ—Person and offices. 3 Apologetics.
I. Title.
BT751.3.J44 2016
234—dc23   2015030758

Published in association with Yates & Yates, www.yates2.com.

16   17   18   19   20   21   22   7   6   5   4   3   2   1

To Donna and Hollis Sullivan

Thank you for your faithful support of Pathway to Victory from its inception as we partner together to share with a lost world that Jesus Christ is the Way, the Truth, and the Life.

Contents

Acknowledgments

I am deeply indebted to the following people who have assisted me in placing this critical message into print:

Brian Vos and the team at Baker Publishing Group, who immediately grasped the significance of this book.

Jennifer Stair, who continues to use her literary skills to assist me in sharpening mine.

Sealy Yates, who has been both my literary agent and trusted adviser for more than twenty years.

Carrilyn Baker, who is the finest executive assistant any pastor could ever hope to work with.

The members of First Baptist Church, Dallas, who encourage their pastor to share the message of Christ to a lost world through any and every platform available.

1

Christianity's Most Offensive Belief

Over the years, I have made frequent appearances on the Fox News show *The O'Reilly Factor*. What I appreciate most about Bill O'Reilly is his willingness to host on his program people with whom he disagrees (such as myself), which explains in part why his show remains the top-rated program in cable news. Although *The O'Reilly Factor* deals primarily with secular subjects, whenever Bill invites me to talk about religious topics the conversation invariably touches on the subject of this book: the exclusivity of Jesus Christ.

In a recent interview about the connection between Islam and terrorism, I recounted the violent track record of Muhammad, the founder of Islam. Bill asked, "How are we supposed to look at Islam? Should we embrace our Muslim brothers and sisters?"

"Absolutely," I said. "I tell my congregation, as individual Christians, we ought to pray for Muslims. We ought to pray and do everything we can to introduce them to faith in Jesus Christ."

I had a feeling my answer might provoke a reaction . . . and it did.

"Are you saying we should proselytize them?" Bill wondered, probably knowing what my response would be.

"Absolutely," I affirmed. "I teach my congregation—"

Bill cut in with another question. "Does that mean doing what you just did, though, nailing Muhammad as a violent guy? Is that the tack you take?" he asked with a smile.

"Well, you have to tell the truth," I said. "And the truth is that Islam is a false religion, built on a false book, written by a false prophet," I explained.[1]

The show was flooded with reactions to the interview—both positive and negative. On the next broadcast, Bill read a viewer's email: "Whenever Pastor Jeffress appears on *The Factor* he sounds reasonable, but then he loses all credibility with me when he insists that his way is the only way to heaven."

O'Reilly accurately responded, "That's what evangelicals believe."[2]

That interview—and reaction to it—was a reminder to me that the single greatest stumbling block for nonbelievers coming to faith in Christ is the issue of exclusivity. You may sound "reasonable" in your explanation of Christianity, but trust me on this: you, too, will lose "all credibility" when you insist that faith in Christ is the only way to heaven.

Are You Ready for the Question?

Even as I am typing these words, I received an email from a church member informing me of a guest he was bringing to dinner for a question-and-answer time with me. "She is not a Christian, because she cannot accept the belief that there is only one way to heaven. Wanted to give you a heads-up so you're ready for her question."

I am ready for the question, primarily because I have spent months researching and writing about this subject. But my purpose in this book is to equip *you* to be ready to articulate and defend this foundational truth of the Christian faith. We must understand the doctrine of the exclusivity of Christ so that we are prepared to respond when people ask us, "Don't all religions lead to heaven?"

The reality of salvation through Christ alone is *not* something we should shy away from in our conversations with unbelievers, thinking it keeps them out of heaven. In contrast, it is the only way for us to invite them in. The most loving thing we can do for our unbelieving family, friends, and people in our circle of influence—for anyone—is to clearly communicate this essential doctrine to them.

> *As Bible-believing Christians, we must be prepared and willing to share the exclusive gospel in our inclusive world.*

As we will see, the answer to the question is, "Not all roads lead to heaven —only the road through saving faith in Jesus Christ does." As Bible-believing Christians, we must be prepared and willing to share the exclusive gospel in our inclusive world.

Clear Answers to Common Questions

Whenever we talk about this issue of the exclusivity of Jesus Christ for salvation, there are several questions that naturally come up, such as "What about all the people who lived before Christ?" and "What happens to young children and mentally challenged adults who are unable to understand the gospel?" and "What about those who have never heard the gospel?" As a pastor, I encounter these questions on a regular basis. And if you've ever had a conversation with unbelieving friends about the subject of salvation through Christ alone, then I bet you've heard these questions too. How should we respond to these questions that so often arise as we are sharing the gospel?

In this book, I will provide you with clear, biblical answers to the seven most common objections to the exclusivity of Christ. The chapters that follow will equip you to help those who are honestly struggling with this truth. However, note that the purpose of this book is not to provide you the ammunition to shoot down unbelievers in a verbal firefight. I have been in enough public debates and heated private conversations with people about spiritual issues to know that it is possible to win a rhetorical battle but lose the spiritual war for a person's eternal soul. Remember, our goal is not to win an argument but to win the other person to faith in God's only way to eternal life in heaven—through Christ alone.

Remember, our goal is not to win an argument but to win the other person to faith in God's only way to eternal life in heaven—through Christ alone.

But before we explore in depth the seven core issues related to the exclusivity of Christ, I first want to address an important, underlying question: Why am I even writing about this topic? Isn't this foundational issue of our faith—that the only way to heaven is through faith in Jesus Christ—something that all Christians already understand and agree on?

Sadly, the answer is no.

In the next chapter, we will discover a startling reason that you and I need to have a very firm grasp on this essential doctrine.

2

Moving the Fence

In many ways, conservative Christians have just about lost the battle over biblical truth. And if we continue making the same strategic mistakes, we are in danger of surrendering the most important issue of our faith.

Consider, as just one example, the issue of gay marriage. I'm among many Christian leaders, lawmakers, and citizens who have fought—and will continue to fight—to retain what the Bible clearly teaches and what has been a widely accepted belief in our country: marriage should be between one man and one woman.

Yet the tide has dramatically and decisively turned against such a so-called restrictive definition of marriage. Since 1996 the percentage of Americans who favor same-sex marriage has more than doubled.[1] Responding to that trend, the Supreme

Court enshrined gay marriage as a civil right on June 26, 2015 (*Obergefell v. Hodges*).

In television debates about the Supreme Court's landmark redefinition of marriage, I often point out, "In 1885 the Supreme Court said in *Murphy v. Ramsey* that marriage is a sacred union between a man and a woman, from which all good things in society come. Now one hundred and thirty years later, the Court changes its mind about the definition of marriage. You have to ask yourself, 'What has changed?' The Constitution hasn't changed. What has changed is the culture. The Supreme Court caved to political correctness."

But it's not just the Supreme Court, liberal activists, or gullible citizens who have buckled under cultural pressure to condone what God has clearly condemned. Christians are increasingly supportive of homosexual unions—especially younger Christians. A recent Pew Religion Forum revealed that 58 percent of young evangelical Christians support some kind of legal recognition of homosexual partnerships.[2]

How can this sea change in opinion among the general population, and especially among Christians, be explained? Not long ago, Cardinal Timothy Dolan of New York claimed in an interview on *Meet the Press* that the church has been "outmarketed" on the issue of gay marriage.[3]

For example, consider how progressives have been able to change the vocabulary: the issue has evolved from "homosexual marriage" to "gay marriage" to "marriage equality." In a country still haunted by its tolerance for racial inequality, who would want to be labeled as a bigot for not supporting "equality" for all people? That's marketing genius! Movies, sitcoms, and newscasts that endlessly stream into American homes have succeeded in not only normalizing homosexual marriage but also marginal-izing those who oppose it as ignorant homophobes who deserve public criticism and shaming.

In addition to being outmarketed in the gay marriage debate, Christians have been *outargued*. A news commentator once ob-served that social conservatives have resorted to Bible-thumping instead of offering a persuasive argument for maintaining the traditional definition of marriage.[4] As someone who "thumps the Bible" regularly for a living, I reluctantly have to agree. Ad-vocates of traditional marriage have been unable to formulate or communicate a convincing case against gay marriage capable of persuading the general public or even the Christian audience.

Most tragically, Christian conservatives have been *outfought* on this issue. We have either laid down our rhetorical weapons and run in retreat, or—even more tragically—we have opened fire on our own troops instead of banding together to fight against untruth.

Last year our church invited a popular sports personality, known for his courage in standing for his Christian faith, to speak to our congregation. When a columnist in New York heard this athlete was coming to our church, he publicly demanded the celebrity cancel his appearance, labeling me as "anti-gay" (because I believe marriage should be between a man and a woman) and "anti-Semitic" (because I preach that Jews, like everyone else, must trust in Christ for salvation). Unable to withstand the pressure, the athlete canceled his appearance at our church. In a phone conversation with me, he acknowledged that he had no disagreements with our church's beliefs (even the liberal *Huffington Post* conceded that our beliefs were "squarely within the mainstream of contemporary right-wing Christian thought"[5]), but said he needed to protect his career and not damage his platform.

A More Crucial Battle

The growing acceptance among Christians of same-sex unions is just one example of how conservative Christians are losing the battle for biblical truth. This issue is sounding the alarm concerning an even more foundational belief that evangelical Christians are in the process of surrendering.

Christians are waffling, wavering, and in the process of ceding the bedrock belief of historic Christianity:

Salvation is only available through faith in Jesus Christ.

You may think I am exaggerating. Are Christians truly abandoning this essential belief? Consider the evidence before you discount the warning. A recent Pew Study revealed that 70 percent of Americans with a religious affiliation say that many religions—not just their own—can lead to eternal life.[6] "That's easily explained," someone might argue. "Almost everyone in America has some religious affiliation, whether they are genuine Christians or not. But surely the statistic among evangelical Christians, who are known for their belief in the Bible, is different." Not by much. A 2008 poll of thirty-five thousand Americans revealed that 57 percent of evangelical church attenders believe that many religions can lead to eternal life.[7]

A few years ago, megachurch pastor Joel Osteen was interviewed by CNN personality Larry King about a variety of subjects. But—as I can attest to from personal experience—it doesn't take long for a non-Christian interviewer to ask an evangelical pastor about the most basic issue of all: Is heaven reserved exclusively for Christians, or are there multiple paths to God? Notice how Osteen answered the question about the eternal fate of non-Christians:

> KING. What if you're Jewish or Muslim, you don't accept Christ at all?
>
> OSTEEN. You know, I'm very careful about saying who would and who wouldn't go to heaven. I don't know. . . .
>
> KING. If you believe you have to believe in Christ? They're wrong, aren't they?
>
> OSTEEN. Well, I don't know if I believe they're wrong. I believe here's what the Bible teaches and from the Christian faith this is what I believe. But I just think that only God will judge a person's heart. I spent a lot of time in India with my father. I don't know all about their religion. But I know they love God. And I don't know. I've seen their sincerity. So I just don't know. I know for me, and what the Bible teaches, I want to have a relationship with Jesus.[8]

I find it interesting that even a person of the Jewish faith like Larry King recognizes the inconsistency in a Christian who claims that faith in Christ is the way to escape God's judgment but there may be other ways to avoid hell as well. If the best answer a prominent pastor like Joel Osteen can give when questioned about the legitimacy of other faiths is, "I don't know. . . . I don't know. . . . I just don't know," then is it any wonder that so many people in evangelical churches are also questioning whether faith in Jesus Christ is the only way a person can be assured of heaven?

What Difference Does It Make?

You may be wondering, *So what if I believe there are multiple paths to God other than Jesus Christ? What difference does it make as long as I trust in Christ for my salvation? Is there any real harm in being tolerant about the possibility that other religions may also lead to salvation?*

In chapter 3, we will explore this question more fully. But to explain why this topic is of critical importance—and why you should keep reading—here is the most convincing reason the issue of the exclusivity of Christ matters:

Your own eternal destiny is at stake.

What you believe about the exclusivity of the gospel of Christ determines whether you will spend eternity in heaven or hell. Perhaps this illustration will help you understand why that's true.

Suppose you come to visit our church in Dallas, Texas. After our service, you decide to drive your rental car down to Houston. However, you mistakenly get on Interstate 75 heading north to Oklahoma. After about an hour, you realize you are on the wrong highway. Interstate 75 will never lead you to Houston, no matter how long you stay on it. Nevertheless, recognizing you are on the wrong highway does not automatically put you on the right road to Houston. Apart from having GPS or a map to guide you, how do you know which of the many roads and highways in Texas will lead you to your desired destination?

The same principle applies when trying to navigate our way to heaven. As we will see in subsequent chapters, Jesus Christ consistently and decisively slammed the door on the idea that all religious paths ultimately lead to eternal life. He declared:

> Enter through the narrow gate; for the gate is wide and the way is broad that leads to destruction, and there are many who enter through it. For the gate is small and the way is narrow that leads to life, and there are few who find it. (Matt. 7:13–14)

Jesus made it very clear exactly what that "small" and "narrow" way is that leads a person to heaven:

> Thomas said to Him, "Lord, we do not know where You are going, how do we know the way?" Jesus said to him, "I am the way, and the truth, and the life; no one comes to the Father but through Me." (John 14:5–6)

Jesus not only declared Himself to be the only way to eternal life but also taught that all other roads lead to eternal destruction. Now, if Jesus was wrong and everyone will eventually arrive in heaven regardless of which road they take, then Christianity cannot be trusted as a reliable highway to heaven. If Jesus was mistaken about this issue, then He could not have been the all-knowing Son of God. And if He wasn't the Son of God, then His death on the cross was not for our sins but for His own. And . . . you get the idea. If Jesus was wrong in His pronouncement about being the only way

If Jesus was wrong in His pronouncement about being the only way to heaven, then the entire Christian faith unravels like a cheap sweater.

to heaven, then the entire Christian faith unravels like a cheap sweater.

So if Jesus Christ is not a reliable way to heaven, then which of the multitude of other spiritual roads do we choose? Because, of all the major religions in the world, only Hinduism teaches that all religions lead to God. In other words, most other faiths claim that *their* way is the exclusive way into the presence of God.

If we embrace the idea that all religions are equally valid, then we are admitting the possibility that Islam, Mormonism, Buddhism, and countless other faiths are correct in teaching that their belief system is the exclusive way to God. So how do we know which of these exclusive spiritual roads to travel to ensure the eternal safety of our souls?

The issue of the exclusivity of the gospel is not just another issue for theologians to wrangle about. Instead, it is key to answering life's most important question: "How can a man be in the right before God?" (Job 9:2). Your answer to that question has significant and eternal consequences for yourself, for your family members and friends, and for the entire world.

Why Are We Losing the Battle?

As we will see in chapters 5 and 6, Jesus and the New Testament writers (most of whom were Jews) consistently taught that faith in Christ is the only means by which anyone can be saved. So why are so many individual believers, pastors, and congregations rejecting this foundational belief and instead embracing pluralism—the idea that all religions are equally valid? Because, as in the example of the gay marriage issue, Christians are being outfought, outargued, and outmarketed when it comes to the issue of salvation through Christ alone. Let's take a closer look at each of these.

Outfought

The issue of the exclusivity of Christ is ground zero of a larger spiritual war between the kingdom of God and the kingdom of Satan. Since the fall of mankind in the garden, the seminal spiritual issue of the ages has been whether people would accept or reject God's plan of redemption.

After realizing the inadequacy of their self-made covering of fig leaves to hide their shame, Adam and Eve received God's offering of a covering He had made from the skin of an innocent animal (Gen. 3:21).

Since that time, the basic question for every person has been, "How will I deal with my sin: by trying to cover it myself or by receiving God's covering?" Some have refused to believe they even need God's forgiveness for their failures. However, the majority of humanity—realizing some need to bridge a separation they feel from God—have chosen to follow the example of Cain. As I explain in detail in chapter 4, instead of following God's prescribed way of forgiveness, this son of the First Couple chose an alternate plan of redemption—one that resulted in God's condemnation (Gen. 4:1–5).

Because we were created as spiritual beings, we feel the need for reconciliation with our Creator. Satan, understanding that need, realizes that the most effective way to prevent people from legitimately connecting with God through faith in Christ is to offer thousands of other alternate roads that falsely promise to lead them to God. For example, if you were stranded in the mountains in the middle of the night looking for a way to safety, a single light that illuminated the path to the highway would be helpful. But a thousand lights would be confusing, especially if nine hundred and ninety-nine of them led you over a cliff.

Don't underestimate Satan's resolve to win this war for the souls of human beings. He is determined to lead as many people as possible off the spiritual cliff to eternal death. Jesus referred to Satan as a murderer and a liar (John 8:44) whose sole purpose is "to steal and kill and destroy" (10:10). Satan's strategy is to confuse and distract people from following the Light of the World, Jesus Christ, by creating a number of other spiritual lights that deceptively offer a way out of humankind's dilemma.

No wonder Paul describes Satan as one who "disguises himself as an angel of light" (2 Cor. 11:14). The apostle goes on to say that Satan accomplishes his spiritual deception through religious people who act as Satan's servants by offering alternate paths to God:

> Therefore it is not surprising if [Satan's] servants also disguise themselves as servants of righteousness, whose end will be according to their deeds. (2 Cor. 11:15)

These servants of Satan who "disguise themselves as servants of righteousness" include:

- the founder of Mormonism, Joseph Smith, who claimed to have received a divine revelation from the angel Moroni.
- the prophet Muhammad, the founder of Islam, who also claimed that an angel spoke to him about the way to ensure eternal life.

- the religious leader wrapped in beautiful clerical robes who says that faith in Christ is important but not sufficient by itself to obtain the forgiveness of sins.
- the evangelical pastor who preaches that although *he* personally believes that Christ offers the way to heaven, sincere followers of other faiths will also be welcomed into God's presence.

The outcome of this battle over the exclusivity of Jesus Christ will affect the eternal destiny of billions of people. I have found that those who want to minimize the importance of this issue are usually oblivious to the reality of spiritual warfare in general. The late pastor Martyn Lloyd-Jones reminds us:

> Not to realize that you are in a conflict means one thing only, and it is that you are so hopelessly defeated, and so "knocked out" as it were, that you do not even know it—you are completely defeated by the devil. Anyone who is not aware of a fight and a conflict in a spiritual sense is in a drugged and hazardous condition.[9]

Millions of Christians are surrendering the core belief in the exclusivity of Christ because they are unaware that this issue is ground zero of the eternal spiritual war between the kingdom of God and the kingdom of Satan. They are not willing to fight to uphold this doctrine because they are in a "drugged and hazardous condition"—induced by a desire for comfort and a disdain for conflict. They don't realize that their surrender will ultimately result in billions of people—including their own friends and family—being deceived by Satan and sentenced to an eternity in hell.

But as we will see, even those Christians who do realize the importance of this issue and are ready to enlist in the battle are regularly being outargued in the public square.

Outargued

Not long ago, I was in a meeting in New York with a senior executive of one of the largest broadcast organizations in the world. He asked me, "With all your responsibilities as the pastor of a large church, why do you spend time talking to the secular media?" I explained that I thought it was important for the Christian worldview to be offered to people for consideration because that point of view was often distorted. For example:

- The issue of the sanctity of life has been turned into "a war on women's health."
- The conviction that marriage should be between a man and a woman has been twisted into "hatred for homosexuals."
- The belief in the freedom of religious expression in the public square has been perverted into "oppression of other religions."
- The good news of God's forgiveness to everyone who trusts in Christ is being rebranded into a "message of intolerance that condemns sincere followers of other faiths."

If we are going to successfully defend this crucial doctrine of the exclusivity of Christ, it is not enough for us to be *willing* to fight; we also need to be *equipped* to fight. That means we need to be armed not only with the truth of God's Word, but like the apostle Paul on Mars Hill (Acts 17), we also need to be equipped with sound logical arguments and easy-to-understand illustrations that will transform Satan's intentional mischaracterization of the gospel as a "message of hate" to a "message of hope."

A few years ago I was on a plane headed to Seattle for an interview for a book I had written. Seated next to me was a well-dressed businessman. As a part of the pre-takeoff chitchat he asked me what I did for a living. Sensing this might be an opportunity to present the gospel, I hedged my answer. After years of experience, I have found that "Southern Baptist pastor" is a real conversation stopper! So I replied, "I am a writer" (which was certainly true).

"What kind of books do you write?" the man inquired.

"I write Christian books," I answered.

"That's interesting. I used to be a Christian," he informed me.

Obviously he was opening the door to an extended conversation, so I asked, "What made you turn away from Christianity?"

"I could no longer accept the idea that there is only one way to heaven. I can't believe in a God so cruel He would torture people for eternity just because they did not believe in Jesus. I can't be a follower of an intolerant religion like that."

I thanked him for his honesty and then proceeded with an illustration. "Suppose this plane were to crash." The flight attendant and passengers across the aisle gave me nasty looks, so I lowered my voice from preacher volume to normal.

"Suppose this plane were to crash," I continued. "The cabin is filling up with smoke. The cabin lights are out and people are groping for a way to exit the burning aircraft. The flight attendant waves her flashlight and says, 'Follow me! There is only one way out of the plane!' Would you accuse her of being hateful for trying to persuade you to follow her directions? Would you label her as 'intolerant' because she claimed there was only one way out of the plane?"

I continued, "Her only motivation for insisting that you follow her directions would be her concern for your safety. The only reason she would insist there is only one safe exit out of the plane would be if indeed there was only one way out of the burning jetliner."

My seatmate nodded as I drove home the point of the analogy. "Our only motivation for trying to convince people to trust in Christ for salvation is a genuine care for their eternal safety. The only reason for insisting that Christ offers the only way to escape eternal death is that all other paths to God are spiritual dead ends."

No, my new acquaintance did not bow his head and pray the sinner's prayer while I softly hummed "Just As I Am." But he did say, "I never thought of it that way before. You've given me a lot to think about."

It's time for us to courageously share the true message of the gospel with others, recognizing that the most loving thing we can do for anyone is to point him or her toward Christ as the only means of eternal salvation.

It is time for those of us who have been entrusted to be "ambassadors for Christ" (2 Cor. 5:20)—not just pastors and missionaries, but every true follower of Christ—to refuse to allow our King's offer of love and redemption to be intentionally mischaracterized as a message of hate and condemnation. It's time for us to courageously share the true message of the gospel with others, recognizing that the most loving thing we can do for anyone is to point him or her toward Christ as the only means of eternal salvation. If you and I give in to the culture's pressure to be "tolerant" and refuse to push back against the enemy's intentional perversion of the gospel, then we are essentially waving the white flag of surrender. And while we remain silent, thousands of people will perish, much like passengers on a burning jetliner who have no one pointing them to the only safe way out.

I can assure you that Satan and his forces are not remaining mute, which is why we are also in danger of being outmarketed by popular celebrities.

Outmarketed

When Jesus described Satan as the "prince of the power of the air" (Eph. 2:2), perhaps the Lord had in mind what Anne Sweeney, president of Disney-ABC Television Group, called "the most powerful medium in the world"—television.[10] The average American watches television five hours a day.[11] When you consider the US population is now more than three hundred million people,[12] the messages that come out of that screen have unlimited potential to shape and transform people's attitudes. And when it comes to the issue of religion, the media is decisively antagonistic about any person or any group who claims their faith offers exclusive truth.

For example, Oprah Winfrey continues to be one of the most powerful figures in broadcasting, and she does not hesitate to use her multifaceted media empire to spread her objection to any religion that claims to be exclusive. "One of the biggest mistakes humans make is to believe there is only one way. Actually, there are many diverse paths leading to what you call God," Oprah opined.[13] Ms. Winfrey is just one of many influential personalities who use the airwaves to spread their message of pluralism. And television is just one communications platform among many—including movies, radio, print, and the internet.

Although Christians are also utilizing these platforms to counter Satan's deceptive message of pluralism, it is almost impossible to compete with and drown out the secularist message of pluralism. The good news is that we don't have to.

The battle over the exclusivity of the gospel of Jesus Christ is not an "air war" but a "ground war." Let me explain. As I type these words I am about to be interviewed about the uniqueness of Jesus Christ on the highest-rated cable news program in the country. However, although several million people will be watching, hundreds of millions of people won't be watching me or anyone else tonight. That is why I am confident that the fight for the very essence of the gospel message is not going to be won by seizing control of the various electronic media available.

For the first two thousand years after Christ's resurrection, the Christian faith exploded from a handful of converts to the most powerful movement the world has ever witnessed. And it happened without the aid of television, radio, or the internet. Instead, the message was carried by "foot soldiers" who were armed with the gospel and ready to share the transforming power of Jesus Christ.

I am not suggesting that Christians should not utilize the various media to broadcast (which means to "broadly cast") Christ's message. Our media ministry, Pathway to Victory, uses television, radio, print, and social media to share the gospel daily with hundreds of millions of people around the world. Every day we hear from people who have come to know Christ through this ministry.

Nevertheless, the most effective marketing plan for the gospel continues to be "equipping of the saints for the work of service, to the building up of the body of Christ" (Eph. 4:12). God's method for communicating His message of redemption to the world is by equipping individual Christians with the gospel message and then sending them into the world, ready to share the gospel on every front: the classroom debate, the break room discussion at work, the conversation with a distraught friend, or the dialogue with the person of another faith. You and I must be ready to communicate the message of the gospel to anyone God brings into our lives. We can use whatever platforms God has given each of us— whether face-to-face communication, phone calls, texting, email, or even social media—to defend and share the good news of Jesus Christ. But in order for us to be properly equipped to fulfill our mission of boldly declaring the gospel through these various outlets, we must first have two essential resources.

First, we must be equipped with *compelling reasoning.* The apostle Peter challenged every Christ follower to always be ready to give an answer to anyone who asks us to give an account for the hope that is in us (1 Pet. 3:15). The most effective resource we have to explain why Jesus Christ is our only hope for salvation is God's Word, which is "sharper than any two-edged sword" and has the capability of piercing Satan's fog of deception that muddles the thinking of non-Christians (Heb. 4:12).

The purpose of this book is not only to convince you that faith in Christ is God's exclusive way to salvation but also to equip you with the biblical basis and logical arguments for communicating that truth to others in a winsome and compelling manner. In the subsequent chapters we will discover:

- what Jesus and the New Testament writers taught about the issue of exclusivity.
- how people who lived before Christ were saved.
- whether those who have never heard of Christ are unjustly sent to hell.
- positive ways to tell people their religion is wrong without sounding hateful.

But well-reasoned rhetoric—even if it is based on God's Word—is not sufficient to win this battle over the exclusivity of Christ.

Second, we must also be equipped with *unwavering resolve.* Don't be surprised at both the overt and subtle pressure you will feel to compromise on this most foundational truth. When I was in high school, I was asked to say the opening prayer at one of our football games since I was the president of the student council. That Friday night we were playing a team from a high school that was largely Jewish. School officials instructed me I was not to offend people by praying in the name of Jesus Christ.

Not knowing what punishment I might face for disobeying the edict, I was faced with the dilemma of whether I was going to please God or please men. Having just sensed God's call to become a pastor, I decided that if I compromised on this issue and denied the only name by which people can be saved, I had no reason for being in the ministry.

Since that Friday night more than forty years ago, I have seen the pressure for Christians to compromise on the exclusivity of Jesus Christ only intensify. That temptation comes in a variety of situations:

- when we consider closing a prayer in a public setting with the words "in Your name" rather than "in Jesus's name" to avoid offending those of different faiths or no faith.

- when we are reluctant to insist in a conversation at work, school, or church that those who fail to trust in Jesus Christ for salvation will be sentenced to eternal separation from God.

- when we are hesitant to go too deep in a conversation with a religious friend or relative about their faith in Jesus Christ, reasoning that various Christian denominations view salvation differently.

A story, perhaps apocryphal, is often told by those who think religion should be inclusive rather than exclusive. During World War I a Protestant chaplain with American soldiers in Italy developed a friendship with a local Roman Catholic priest. Eventually, the chaplain moved on with his unit and was killed. The priest heard of his death and asked military authorities if the chaplain could be buried in the cemetery behind his church. Permission was granted.

But the priest ran into a problem with his own Catholic church authorities. They were sympathetic with his desire, but they could not approve the burial of a non-Catholic in a Catholic cemetery. So the priest buried his friend just outside the cemetery fence.

Many years later, a friend of the chaplain who knew what had happened returned to Italy and visited the old priest. The first thing he did was to ask to see the chaplain's grave. To his surprise, he found the grave inside the fence. "Oh," he said, "I see you got permission to move the body."

"No," said the priest. "They told me where I couldn't bury the body. But nobody ever told me I couldn't move the fence."

Christians are increasingly being bullied by those outside the faith and badgered by many within the Christian camp to be more inclusive about who will populate heaven. The problem is that none of us has either the right or the ability to "move the fence" or broaden the road that leads to heaven. For as Jesus Himself said, "The gate is small and the way is narrow that leads to life, and there are few who find it" (Matt. 7:14).

In the pages ahead we will discover what that "way" is that leads to eternal life and why the most loving thing you can do for anyone is to point him or her toward it. But first, we will address one of the most common questions you will hear from skeptics whenever the conversation turns to the message of salvation: Does it really matter?

3

Does It Really Matter?

"Dr. Jeffress, I'm considering having my body cremated when I die, but some of my Christian friends are telling me that cremation is wrong. What do you think?" a listener to our radio program recently inquired. I can sense that many of you reading these words have what you are confident is the *right* answer to that inquiry. My response? "Worms or fire, take your pick; the result is the same. Your body is going to disintegrate—cremation only accelerates the process."

Every day my email in-box reminds me of the diversity of beliefs on a wide variety of topics among evangelical Christians who believe in the inspiration and authority of the Bible:

- Will Christians be raptured before the Great Tribulation or will they be forced to endure it?

- Are some people predestined by God to be saved while others are predestined to be condemned for all eternity?
- Are the six days of creation actual twenty-four-hour periods of time or are they representative of longer periods of time?
- Is Paul's restriction of women from pastoral leadership positions limited to his culture or does it apply universally to today?
- Is the gift of tongues still operational today?
- Should Christians drink alcohol?

If you are under the illusion that there is any unity among Christians on these hot-button issues, then I invite you to throw out any of the above questions in your next small-group meeting at church and sit back and listen! You will be amazed not only at the lack of consensus among your fellow Christians on these issues but the vigorous—often bordering on vitriolic—passion with which they will argue their point of view.

How is it that sincere Christians who are indwelled by the same Holy Spirit of God and read the same Bible do not arrive at the same conclusions? The limitations of human understanding, the impact of culture, and the influence of our particular faith tradition or personal experiences all shape our interpretation of Scripture, whether we are willing to admit it or not. That is why a maxim often attributed to seventeenth-century theologian Rupert Meldenius should guide our interactions with other Christians regarding controversial topics: "In essentials, unity; in nonessentials, liberty; and in all things, charity."

But when we are confronted by the question, "Is personal faith in Jesus Christ the only way a person can be saved from God's condemnation?" we must determine whether this question is essential or nonessential. If the exclusivity of the gospel of Jesus Christ is in the same category as the age of the earth or the propriety of cremation, then we should acknowledge our own opinion but also respect other points of view and together agree that no one's eternal destiny hinges on the issue.

However, as I claimed in the previous chapter, the exclusivity of Jesus Christ for salvation is not a secondary or tertiary issue; it represents the core of the Christian message. Our eternal destiny—and the eternal destiny of our friends and loved ones, as well as every single person on earth—rests squarely on this foundational truth. As pastor and author John Piper writes, "My sense of urgency increases the more I think about what is at stake in surrendering the universal necessity of believing on Jesus in order to be saved."[1]

Nevertheless, the exclusivity of Christ is an issue over which Christians are increasingly divided. Author Ronald Nash observes:

> Once upon a time Christians were identifiable by an unqualified commitment to Jesus Christ as the one and only Savior of the world. But the unity of Christians on this fundamental issue has disappeared. Today many people who claim to be Christians choose among three fundamentally different answers to the question, "Is Jesus the only Savior?" These answers can be stated succinctly: No! Yes, but . . . Yes, period![2]

Several national polls on this subject confirm Nash's claim. According to a survey conducted by the Barna Group in 2011,

40 percent of Americans surveyed agreed with the statement, "All people are eventually saved or accepted by God, no matter what they do, because he loves all people he has created."[3] Of course, that figure includes people of all religions and even atheists. Yet the same poll revealed that 26 percent of those identifying themselves as born-again Christians agreed with the statement: "It doesn't matter what religious faith you follow because they all teach the same lessons."[4] As mentioned in chapter 2, a poll of thirty-five thousand Americans discovered that 57 percent of evangelical church attenders said they believe that many religions can lead to eternal life.[5] The staggering reality is that you are just as likely to hear the casual remark "All religions are the same, so why does it matter?" from the person sitting next to you at church as you are from unbelievers at a neighborhood gathering or in a secular classroom.

You might think that it is only the atheists, heretics, and liberal theologians who reject the belief that personal faith in Christ is necessary for salvation—but you would be wrong. Noted Christian writer C. S. Lewis believed that heaven includes people who have never exercised faith in Christ. He wrote:

> I think that every prayer which is sincerely made even to a false god or to a very imperfectly conceived true God, is accepted by the true God and that Christ saves many who do not think they know Him.[6]

If such a renowned apologist for the Christian faith as C. S. Lewis believed there are other ways for a person to be saved apart from personal faith in Christ, then is it possible that historic Christianity has indeed been guilty of proclaiming an unnecessarily exclusive and intolerant message?

Four Answers

Who will be in heaven? Before we begin to answer that question, it might be helpful to define four terms that represent four different answers to it.

Universalism

Universalism is the belief that everyone, regardless of his or her belief or unbelief, will be accepted by God for all eternity. This view affirms that all people will be ultimately saved and that no one will experience God's punishment. Former pastor Rob Bell popularized this concept a few years ago in his highly controversial book *Love Wins*:

> Millions have been taught that if they don't believe, if they don't accept in the right way according to the person telling them the gospel, and they were hit by a car and died later that same day, God would have no choice but to punish them forever in conscious torment in hell. . . .
>
> A loving heavenly father who will go to extraordinary lengths to have a relationship with them would, in the blink of an eye, become a cruel, mean, and vicious tormenter who would ensure that they would have no escape from an endless future of agony.
>
> If there was an earthly father who was like that, we would call the authorities. . . . That kind of God is simply devastating. Psychologically crushing. We can't bear it. . . . That God is terrifying and traumatizing and unbearable.[7]

Bell's flawed logic ("If I can't conceive of a God who would eternally punish unbelievers, then that kind of God must not exist") leads him to surmise that people who are relegated to hell (whatever that is) will only temporarily reside there and will ultimately be redeemed:

> No one can resist God's pursuit forever because God's love will eventually melt even the hardest hearts.[8]

Some universalists (called inclusivists) maintain that all people will be saved based on the death of Christ on the cross, which they say resulted in salvation for all mankind. However, the majority of universalists reject the biblical concept of sin that would necessitate the sacrificial death of the Son of God.

Pluralism

Pluralism restricts salvation to religious people, regardless of what that religion is. This belief maintains that all religions are equally valid, picturing the variety of world religions as different paths up the same mountain that lead ultimately to the same God. Certainly this view is appealing given the number of adherents to religions other than Christianity.

According to the *World Christian Encyclopedia*, the world is populated by about 1 billion Muslims, 650 million Hindus, over 300 million Buddhists, and over 200 million followers of Chinese folk religion, not to mention the almost 2 billion people who claim to be Christians.[9] And today, those adherents of non-Christian religions are no longer relegated to faraway countries most Americans cannot locate on a map. Instead, followers of these religions reside in our cities and neighborhoods. Their mosques, temples, and worship centers stand alongside our churches and synagogues.

As our country becomes increasingly diverse, pluralism becomes increasingly popular. Unlike universalism, pluralism doesn't require us to allow murderers and drug dealers into heaven, as pluralists still restrict the population of heaven to religious people. But adopting pluralism allows us to appear more tolerant and eliminates the necessity of judging someone else's religion as "wrong."

Inclusivism

Inclusivism holds that the sacrificial death of Christ on the cross is the only means by which people can be saved. However, inclusivism also says that a person can be saved by Christ without ever personally believing in Christ. In other words, the death of Christ was sufficient to save a group of people larger than those who have heard and believed in Jesus Christ.

Perhaps the best way to understand this view is to contrast it with the other viewpoints about salvation we have just explored. Universalism maintains that all people will go to heaven regardless of their beliefs or unbelief. Pluralism narrows salvation to religious people but says that all religions are equally capable of offering salvation.

However, inclusivism affirms that no one can be saved apart from the work of Jesus Christ on the cross. Adherents of this view would have no trouble agreeing with the apostle Peter's declaration to the Jewish authorities:

> There is salvation in no one else; for there is no other name under heaven that has been given among men by which we must be saved. (Acts 4:12)

Inclusivists do not claim that everyone will be saved, as universalists do. And unlike pluralists, inclusivists do not maintain that

Islam, Judaism, and Hinduism are equally valid religions. Most inclusivists would shout a hearty amen to Jesus's claim in John 14:6: "I am the way, and the truth, and the life; no one comes to the Father but through Me." But inclusivists believe the circle of salvation is wider than only those who have personally trusted in Jesus Christ as their Savior. For example, inclusivists argue that those who have never heard the gospel but believe in the limited revelation of God they have received will be in heaven. Inclusivists also include in the population of heaven followers of other religions whom they insist are simply "calling Jesus by another name."

You might wonder whom inclusivists believe would *not* be saved. Most believers in inclusivism limit the occupants of hell to those who have received and willfully rejected God's message of redemption, however complete or incomplete that message was. For example:

- In the days of Noah, it would be those who heard Noah's warning of judgment but refused to take refuge in the ark, thus experiencing God's condemnation.
- In the days of the Mosaic law, it would be those who heard the law but refused to follow God's commands and offer the prescribed sacrifices.
- In the days when Jesus walked the earth, it would be those who heard Jesus's claims but rejected Christ as Messiah and faced eternal condemnation.
- In America today, it would be those who have heard the gospel message repeatedly but have hardened their hearts against it.
- In remote villages around the globe where the name of Jesus has never been heard, it would be those who refuse

to respond to the limited knowledge of God they have received through creation.

However, inclusivism maintains that anyone who has ever demonstrated a sincere desire to know God and has embraced rather than rejected whatever information he or she has received about God will be accepted by God. The basis of that seeker's salvation is the sacrificial death of Jesus Christ for his or her sins, even though the seeker may be oblivious to that act. John Sanders, a proponent of inclusivism, writes:

> It is not certain . . . that one must hear of Christ in this life to obtain salvation. [New Testament passages] simply say there is no other way one can get to heaven except through the work of Christ; they do not say one has to know about that work in order to benefit from the work.[10]

In other words, you can receive the gift of salvation without ever knowing the identity of the sender of the gift, the inclusivist argues.

Exclusivism

Exclusivism is the view that salvation is limited to those who exercise personal faith in Jesus Christ as their Savior. Unlike universalists, exclusivists believe many—actually, most—people will be condemned to an eternity in hell. Unlike pluralists, exclusivists believe that hell will be populated by sincere followers of other religions.

Like inclusivists, exclusivists also maintain that no one can be saved apart from the sacrificial death of Jesus Christ on the cross. But the major contrast between inclusivism and exclusivism is this: exclusivists believe that since the time of Christ's death, individuals in every generation and in every culture must personally trust in Jesus Christ as Savior in order to be in a right relationship with God. (The two exceptions to this principle for most exclusivists would be children too young to understand the gospel and mentally challenged people who cannot understand the gospel. We will discuss these exceptions in detail in chapter 8.)

Exclusivists point to numerous passages in the New Testament that connect eternal salvation with personal belief:

> For God so loved the world, that He gave His only begotten Son, that whoever believes in Him shall not perish, but have eternal life. (John 3:16)

> I am the resurrection and the life; he who believes in Me will live even if he dies, and everyone who lives and believes in Me will never die. Do you believe this? (John 11:25–26)

> They said, "Believe in the Lord Jesus, and you will be saved, you and your household." (Acts 16:31)

> If you confess with your mouth Jesus as Lord, and believe in your heart that God raised Him from the dead, you will be saved. (Rom. 10:9)

Jesus, the apostle Paul, and other New Testament writers repeatedly emphasize the importance of personal belief in order to be saved. Obviously, this viewpoint raises a number of interesting—if not troubling—questions:

- "What about those who have never heard the gospel of Jesus Christ? It is unfair for God to condemn people for not accepting a message they have never heard."

- "What about people who lived in the time before Christ? If Abraham, Moses, David, and a multitude of Jews and gentiles were saved apart from a personal belief in the sacrificial death of Christ, then why shouldn't we believe there are alternative ways of salvation today?"

- "Is it reasonable to believe that a good, moral Muslim who sincerely worships the god he calls Allah will be sent to hell, while a mass murderer who professes faith in Christ immediately before his execution will spend eternity in heaven? How could a God of justice ever do such a thing?"

In subsequent chapters, we will explore the Bible's very clear—though not always easy to accept—answers to those questions. But before we do, it is important to answer the foundational question posed in the title of this chapter: Does it really matter whether personal faith in Christ is the only way by which a person can be saved—and if so, why?

Why It Matters

What's the harm in being tolerant of other religions and spiritual paths? Why does it matter whether we compromise a little bit on the truth that Jesus Christ is the only way to heaven?

Consider a long row of dominoes. Just as the toppling of the first domino in a line begins a chain reaction of collapsing dominoes behind it, one event often sets in motion a chain of continuing consequences.

I believe there are six "dominoes" lined up behind the issue of the exclusivity of the gospel of Jesus Christ that logically collapse if we allow this crucial doctrine to fall.

The Nature of Truth

Are there universal principles that transcend time and culture, or is all truth relative to the time and culture in which a person lives? George Barna revealed some years ago that 68 percent of adults who claimed to be born-again Christians and 91 percent of Christian teenagers rejected the concept of absolute truth and instead embraced relativism—a concept best explained by the phrase "Everything is right sometime, and nothing is right every time."[11]

This rejection of the concept (much less the application) of absolute truth explains why increasing numbers of Christians accept homosexual marriage, engage in unbiblical divorce, and participate in unethical behavior. But the wholesale embracing of relativism also explains why so many Christians do not believe that Christ is the exclusive way of salvation.

I remember hearing a well-known evangelical Christian speaking at a memorial service that included people of diverse faith backgrounds. In what I suppose was an attempt to demonstrate sensitivity for non-Christians in attendance that day, the speaker mentioned Jesus Christ, adding "and for those of us who are Christians, He is the Savior of the world." While some might applaud the speaker's boldness in making such a declaration, the truth is that he diluted the gospel message by implying the gospel is true only for those who believe it is true.

Faith in Jesus Christ as Savior as the exclusive way of salvation is an absolute truth for all people.

Such a declaration would be tantamount to saying, "The law of gravity only applies to those who believe in the law of gravity." Really? If you jump off a thirty-story building, you are going to splatter on the sidewalk whether or not you personally believe in gravity! Similarly, the "law of exclusivity" applies to everyone, not just to Christians who believe in it. Faith in Jesus Christ as Savior as the exclusive way of salvation is an absolute truth for all people.

The Bible

A recent survey by George Gallup revealed that while 75 percent of Americans believe that the Bible is the "inspired Word of God," only 28 percent believe that the Bible can be taken "literally"—an all-time low in more than thirty years.[12] I realize *literally* is both an imprecise and loaded term. For example, no sane person believes that when Jesus said, "I am the door" (John 10:9), He was claiming to have hinges and a doorknob. Jesus was using a metaphor to describe Himself.

However, the theological imprecision of this poll question should not be allowed to mask the reality that an increasing number of unbelievers and believers reject the absolute authority of the Bible on issues of faith and practice. Our ever-changing world causes us to ask ourselves the same question the serpent posed to Eve: "Indeed, has God said . . . ?" (Gen. 3:1). It's important to note that the serpent (in the beginning, at least) did not attempt to contradict God by saying, "Eve, God was wrong when He said not to eat of this tree." The serpent was forced to use that line of attack only after Eve affirmed her belief that she had indeed heard and interpreted God's words accurately.

However, for most of the rest of us, Satan never has to actually declare God to be a liar. He simply needs to make us question whether the Bible is God's inspired Word to us and if we have interpreted it correctly:

- "Given the abundance of evidence for evolution, has God really said that He formed man out of the dust of the earth?"
- "Given the number of people who are drawn to same-sex relationships, has God really said that marriage should be restricted to a man and a woman?"
- "Given the prevalence of different religions in the world, has God really said that Christianity offers the only way to heaven?"

If we allow the culture to pressure us to concede the historic doctrine of the exclusivity of Christ, then we will be allowing for a further diminution of the trustworthiness and authority of the Scriptures.

The Deity of Jesus Christ

The doctrine of Christ's divinity stands or falls on this issue of the exclusivity of Christ for salvation. How can I make such a sweeping claim? Just consider some of Jesus's comments about this subject that leave no doubt where He stood on the issue.

Jesus rejected the idea that everyone would be saved (universalism): "For the gate is small and the way is narrow that leads to life, and there are few who find it" (Matt. 7:14).

Jesus denied that all belief systems offer an equally valid way to God (pluralism): "I am the way, and the truth, and the life; no one comes to the Father but through Me" (John 14:6).

Jesus refused the view that personal faith isn't necessary to obtain eternal life (inclusivism): "For this is the will of My Father, that everyone who beholds the Son and believes in Him will have eternal life, and I Myself will raise him up on the last day" (John 6:40).

As I will detail in chapter 5, Jesus was the primary proponent of exclusivism in the New Testament. If the universalists, pluralists, or inclusivists are right, then Jesus was wrong in His numerous declarations that faith in Him is the only path that leads to heaven. If Jesus was wrong, then it was because He was either mistaken or intentionally misleading. If Jesus was mistaken, then He was not omniscient (all-knowing) and therefore was not God. If He was being intentionally misleading, then He was not holy and therefore was not God. Either way, the doctrine of Christ's deity rests on the issue of exclusivity.

The Necessity of the Atonement

On a recent trip to Israel, I took our group of travelers into the Garden of Gethsemane, where Jesus prayed fervently just before His arrest, trials, and execution. Before we divided up to find our own places of solitude to talk with our heavenly Father, I read aloud from Luke's account of that gut-wrenching ordeal for Jesus:

> He withdrew from them about a stone's throw, and He knelt down and began to pray, saying, "Father, if You are willing, remove this cup from Me; yet not My will, but Yours be done." Now an angel from heaven appeared to Him, strengthening Him. And being in agony He was praying very fervently; and His sweat became like drops of blood, falling down upon the ground. (Luke 22:41–44)

When you think of Jesus praying in the garden perhaps you picture Him striking a dignified, ministerial pose as He kneels beside a large rock with His head resting against His folded arms, as some artists have rendered the event. In reality, Jesus was so "distressed and troubled" (Mark 14:33) that as He was walking through Gethsemane He collapsed and begin to cry out to God to deliver Him from the horrible experience that was before Him (vv. 35–36).

Certainly Jesus would have been justified in asking His heavenly Father to spare Him from the horrendous and sadistic method of execution the Romans had devised. But what terrified Jesus more than the physical agony of the cross was the spiritual consequence of paying for the sins of all humanity—experiencing the full fury of God's wrath rather than God's complete and eternal delight in the Son with whom He was well pleased.

From all eternity past, Jesus had never experienced anything but complete harmony with His Father. But that was about to change. God the Father was about to turn His back on the Son who had brought the Father nothing but sheer delight. I have a friend who told me about the day when he was nine years old and his father walked into his room and said he was disowning him. His dad informed him that he was going to change his name and never have any contact with his son again. More than half a century later my friend has still not completely recovered from that horrible experience.

That night in Gethsemane Jesus knew He was about to face a more temporary but no less painful estrangement from His Father for bearing the sins of the world—an experience that would later cause Him to cry out from the cross, "My God, My God, why have You forsaken Me?" (Matt. 27:46).

It is no wonder that Jesus would plead with God in the garden to spare Him from the horrific experience of the cross and find some other way to accomplish the need for humanity's forgiveness and restoration. But God responded to His Son's fervent request with thundering silence. God offered no other way, because there was no other way for humanity's redemption.

Now here's the point: if the universalists are correct that everyone will go to heaven and no one will be judged, then Christ's horrific experience was unfortunate. If the pluralists are correct that every religion offers an equally valid pathway to God, then Christ's sacrificial death was unnecessary. If either of these viewpoints were true, then God sending His Son to die on a cross was not only unbearably cruel but also completely useless.

However, Scripture assures us that Jesus's crucifixion permanently altered the eternal destiny of all those who place their faith in Him. The apostle John, who witnessed Christ's agony on the cross, wrote many years later about what Christ accomplished by His death: "He Himself is the propitiation for our sins" (1 John 2:2).

The word *propitiation* means "appeasement" or "satisfaction." Pagan religions in some parts of the world during John's time taught that the only way to satisfy the requirements of the angry gods was by participating in endless religious rituals or offering children as burnt offerings. Today other religions such as Buddhism and Hinduism identify different human foibles we need to correct in order to please the gods or at least enjoy a fuller life. Islam and Judaism mandate adherence to a list of dos and don'ts to satisfy their God.

But these various religions all share a common denominator: it is man who is responsible for appeasing God or the gods through rituals, self-improvement, or rule keeping. However, the unique message of Christianity is that Jesus Christ alone

When people reject the belief that faith in Christ is the exclusive way for a person to be saved, they are radically changing the meaning and necessity of Christ's death.

is capable of offering a sufficient sacrifice to atone for (the word *atone* means "cover") our sins that have offended a holy God.

When people reject the belief that faith in Christ is the exclusive way for a person to be saved, they are radically changing the meaning and necessity of Christ's death. If it is possible for us to be in a right relationship with God automatically (universalism) or through any number of different religions (pluralism), then Christ's death was no more than an example of selflessness and was certainly not absolutely necessary to cover our sins.

The Reality of Hell

Another theological "domino" that falls when the exclusivity of Christ is rejected is the doctrine of eternal punishment for those who reject the message of Christ. If the universalists are correct that every person goes to heaven, then the only occupants of hell will be Satan and the angels who chose to follow him (Matt. 25:41). If the pluralists are correct that all religions offer equally valid ways to heaven, then hell will be populated only with the most hardened atheists who have rejected belief in any god. If the inclusivists are correct that Christ's death automatically covered the sins of those who have never heard of Him and therefore never believed in Him, then the number of people in hell will be relatively miniscule compared to the number of people in heaven.

The problem with all of these views is that they contradict what Jesus Christ taught about the population count in hell. Jesus warned:

> Enter through the narrow gate; for the gate is wide and the way is broad that leads to destruction, and there are many who enter through it. For the gate is small and the way is narrow that leads to life, and there are few who find it. (Matt. 7:13–14)

If universalism, pluralism, or inclusivism is true, then Jesus should revise His above statement to read:

> Enter through the wide gate; for the gate is narrow and the way is small (or nonexistent) that leads to destruction, and there are few who enter through it. For the gate is wide and the way is broad that leads to life, and most, if not everyone, will find it.

Of course, that is not what Jesus said. In chapter 5 we will explore more fully Jesus's teachings about heaven and hell.

Evangelism and Missions

Christ's final marching orders to His followers were for them to go into all the world and "make disciples" (Matt. 28:19–20). If I had been one of those disciples and believed that faith in Christ was nice but not absolutely necessary to obtain eternal life, I would have raised my hand and politely asked the Lord, "Why?"

Why go to the trouble of traveling to the "remotest part of the earth" (Acts 1:8) or even walking across the street to share Christ if everyone is going to heaven anyway, as the universalists claim?

Why offend someone of a different religion and risk being perceived as arrogant if in fact his or her religion is just as capable of leading him or her to heaven as Christianity, as the pluralists claim?

Why travel (or sacrifice to provide funds for others to travel) to distant countries to share the gospel with those who have never heard about Jesus if everyone is automatically assured of heaven based on the death of Christ, as the inclusivists claim? In fact, since inclusivists limit hell only to those who have heard and then actively rejected the gospel, don't unbelievers in other countries—or even this country—who have never heard the gospel stand a better chance of going to heaven if they never hear about Christ rather than hearing the gospel and then rejecting it?

Only those who believe that personal faith in Jesus Christ is absolutely necessary for salvation have any logical reason to share their faith with others. Universalism, pluralism, and even inclusivism are all attempts to deny—or at least temper—the bad news: everyone who fails to accept Christ's offer of forgiveness is destined to be eternally separated from God. And to the degree to which a worldview denies the bad news, it diminishes the imperative of sharing the good news (the literal meaning of *gospel*).

Hopefully, you now see why the doctrine of exclusivity is not a secondary issue but is intricately connected to other foundational beliefs of the Christian faith. It is an essential truth that should not only affect our own eternal destiny but also motivate us to share the message of the gospel with those who are being deceived by the culture's lies.

But an equally strong argument for the exclusivity of Christ is this doctrine's connection to the character of God as first revealed in the Old Testament. As we will see in the next chapter, from the opening pages of Genesis God has insisted that there is only one way to approach Him.

4

The Old Way Was One Way

My friend David Jeremiah tells about a woman who approached him after a sermon, protesting, "My God would never send someone to hell for simply not believing in Jesus."

"You're right," David said to the somewhat surprised woman. "Your God wouldn't do that . . . because He doesn't exist." As one wag has noted, "In the beginning God created man in His own image, and ever since that time man has tried to return the favor."

Many of us are guilty of creating and serving the God we wish existed rather than the God who actually exists. The disparity between the two can spell the difference between eternal life and eternal death. That is why A. W. Tozer wrote, "What comes into our minds when we think about God is the most important thing about us."[1] To put a finer point on Tozer's claim: it is crucial that when we contemplate God, we think about the true God who rules over creation rather than the god who resides in our imagination.

If the true God issues declarations and commands, then they are absolute. If an imaginary god issues declarations and commands, then they are inconsequential.

If the true God mandates what He requires from me, then I had better listen. If an imaginary god makes a demand I dislike, then I can create a different god in my mind.

If the true God claims there is only one way to experience eternal life, then I want to be sure I discover it. If an imaginary god makes such a claim, then I can easily ignore it.

I love the story about the first grader in Sunday school who was working hard on a drawing. His teacher asked, "What are you drawing?" "Oh, I'm drawing a picture of God," the boy responded. The teacher gently explained, "Since no one has seen God, no one knows what He looks like." The first grader confidently replied, "They will now!"

While it is true that no one has seen God the Father, there is a great deal we can know about Him: His likes and dislikes, His character, His commands, His thoughts about us, His purpose for the world, and His plans for us in this life and in the life to come. Where do we go to find this information? It is all deposited in the Bible.

The foundational assumption of everything I say in this book is that the Bible is God's perfect revelation to us and can be trusted to tell us the truth about every subject it addresses, including the only way we can experience eternal life. I understand that not everyone reading this book agrees with that statement. While the evidence for the reliability of the Bible is beyond the scope of this book, let me assure you that you do not have to commit intellectual suicide to believe the Bible is uniquely inspired by God and can be trusted in everything it says. There is strong historical, archaeological, literary, and prophetic evidence that the Bible is God's authoritative Word to us.[2]

If we accept the proposition that the Bible is God's unique message to us, then we can believe everything that God reveals about Himself in the Scriptures—and the beginning point of that revelation is the Old Testament.

Many people have difficulty knowing how to interpret the Old Testament. One of the questions I'm often asked by the secular media is why Christians embrace some of the Old Testament and reject other portions of it. For example, the majority of Christians believe that the prohibition against homosexuality found in Leviticus 18:22 applies today as well: "You shall not lie with a male as one lies with a female; it is an abomination." Yet I don't know of any Christians who believe that the command in Leviticus 19:19 is relevant for today:

> You are to keep My statutes. You shall not breed together two kinds of your cattle; you shall not sow your field with two kinds of seed, nor wear a garment upon you of two kinds of material mixed together.

On what basis do we denounce homosexual activity while wearing clothing with a cotton/polyester blend?

The simple answer is that the only commands found in the Old *Testament* (a word meaning "covenant" or "agreement") that are applicable to us today are those commands that are repeated in the New Testament. For example, the prohibitions against homosexuality, adultery, lying, and murder are all restated in the New Testament. However, you cannot find any prohibitions in the New Testament against breeding two kinds of cattle or sowing two kinds of seed in the same field.

Why Read the Old Testament?

"Then what is the value of reading the Old Testament at all?" you may ask. Trust me, I ask myself that same question when my Read Through the Bible program lands me in the middle of Leviticus. J. I. Packer, in his landmark book *Knowing God,* asked a similar question when he noted that the people, culture, and customs of the Old Testament seem very strange to us. How can those of us living in the twenty-first century ever relate to those living during Old Testament times? Packer answers his own question with a statement I have never forgotten since I first read it as a teenager:

> It is true that in terms of space, time, and culture, they [those living in the Old Testament] and the historical epoch to which they belonged are a very long way away from us. But the link between them and us is not found at that level.
>
> The link is God himself. For the God with whom they had to do is the same God with whom we have to do.[3]

The unifying bridge between the people in the Old Testament with strange customs and unpronounceable names and us is God. He remains the same yesterday, today, and forever (Heb. 13:8). That means that the question we should be constantly asking ourselves when we read the Old Testament is "What does this passage teach me about the character of God?" Unfortunately, many unbelievers and believers alike have decided that the Old Testament does not teach us anything worthwhile—or true—about God. In his book *The God Delusion*, Oxford biologist Richard Dawkins writes:

> The God of the Old Testament is arguably the most unpleasant character in all of fiction: jealous and proud of it; a petty, unjust, unforgiving control-freak; a vindictive, bloodthirsty ethnic cleanser; a misogynistic, homophobic, racist, infanticidal, genocidal, filicidal, pestilential, megalomaniacal, sadomasochistic, capriciously malevolent bully.[4]

It is not only virulent atheists like Dawkins who find the God described in the Old Testament repugnant. Many professing Christians have bought into the false dichotomy between the God of the Old Testament and the God of the New Testament personified in Jesus Christ. I will never forget, when I was a student at a Baptist college, hearing my Old Testament religion teacher (who had also been pastor of a prominent Baptist church) make this comment: "The Bible is simply a collection of men's ideas about God. In the Old Testament you find man's worst thoughts about God: a bloodthirsty deity who constantly sought revenge. In the New Testament you find man's loftiest ideas of God as exemplified in Jesus." This is a common mind-set today among Christians and skeptics alike.

Yet the truth is that the New Testament does not present a one-dimensional God whose only attribute is love. The same Jesus who declared that "God so loved the world, that He gave His only begotten Son" (John 3:16) is also returning in judgment to "strike down the nations, and . . . rule them with a rod of iron [as] He treads the wine press of the fierce wrath of God, the Almighty" (Rev. 19:15).

Similarly, the Old Testament reveals more about God than just His anger against evildoers. From Genesis to Malachi we also find a God who is described as "compassionate and gracious, slow to anger and abounding in lovingkindness" (Ps. 103:8).

You may wonder what all of this has to do with the subject of this book. The answer is everything. If the Bible is simply a collection of contradictory ideas about God, then which God should we listen to and attempt to please: the angry, unreasonable God of the Old Testament who appears to hate everyone or the loving God of the New Testament who judges no one? In the first case, who would want to share the message of a God who is bad-tempered and impossible to please? In the second case, if God is so loving that He simply accepts everyone as they are, then why bother sharing the gospel since God won't judge people anyway?

In truth, both the Old and New Testaments reveal to us a variety of aspects of the same God "with whom we have to do" (Heb. 4:13). He is both loving and just. His righteousness demands that He punish sin, but His love motivates Him to offer a way to forgive sinners.

Five Themes of Exclusivity in the Old Testament

When it comes to the question of whether God has provided multiple paths to heaven, the consistent message of the Old Testament is that there is only one way a person can ever be in a right relationship with God. The Old Testament message of exclusivity can be clearly seen in five themes found in the Old Testament.

The Oneness of God

Ask most Christians today to name the most important verse in the Bible and they would probably cite John 3:16: "For God so loved the world, that He gave His only begotten Son, that whoever believes in Him shall not perish, but have eternal life." However, if you were to ask an Israelite living in Old Testament times the same question, he would quickly answer with Deuteronomy 6:4: "Hear, O Israel! The LORD is our God, the LORD is one!" If football had existed then, you would have seen that verse on banners throughout the stadium. This verse represented the core belief of the Israelites—a belief that distinguished Judaism from other popular religions of the day.

Remember the setting for this verse. After forty years of wandering in the wilderness, the Israelites were now ready to enter the Promised Land of Canaan that was inhabited by— you guessed it— Canaanites. Through His prophet Moses, God warned the Israelites about some of the temptations they would face from their soon-to-be new neighbors. The Canaanites engaged in every kind of debauchery imaginable —and unimaginable.

But their basic problem was that they did not revere the true God. Instead, they recognized a multitude of different gods who were often at odds with one another. The pagan worshiper had to choose which god to follow without ever being sure he or she had chosen the right god.

But in his farewell message to his spiritual children, Moses reminded the Israelites that there is only one legitimate God.

- He is the God whom Moses had met for the first time eighty years earlier on Mount Horeb.
- He is the God who appeared to Moses as a blazing fire in a burning bush and called Moses by name.
- He is the God who called Himself "I Am Who I Am."

Notice God didn't call Himself "I Am Whoever You Think I Am." God reminded Moses that He possessed definite characteristics and had a definitive plan for Moses.

When I am in a public setting, like standing in the concession line at a movie theater talking to my family, I am occasionally approached by someone who says, "I recognize your voice. You're that guy on the radio, aren't you?" More than once, what follows is not the compliment I had hoped for but the observation, "You don't look anything like I imagined. You are _____ (older, shorter, grayer, etc.) than I imagined." The operative word here is *imagined*. I am not the sum of people's speculations about me—and neither are you. Neither is God. He is who He is.

The Holiness of God

If you asked your best friend to describe you, he or she would probably list a number of characteristics, some of which might even seem contradictory but which taken together offer an accurate picture of who you are. Yet you are more than all the words your friend uses to describe you. While there are a number of people who possess the same characteristics as you, there is no one in the world who is identical to you. You are unique.

God also possesses a number of attributes. He is omniscient (all-knowing), omnipotent (all-powerful), just, loving, purposeful, and so on. But the one attribute that transcends all others is *holy*. When the prophet Isaiah saw the vision of God on His throne, he heard the angels crying out, "Holy, Holy, Holy is the LORD of hosts" (Isa. 6:3). The angels did *not* cry out "Love, love, love," or "Just, Just, Just," or "Omnipotent, omnipotent,

omnipotent" (which would have been quite a tongue twister). Why not?

While each of those attributes describes an aspect of God's being, none of those words paints the complete picture of who He is. There really is only one word that can describe the totality of God's being: *holy*. The word translated "holy" comes from a Hebrew word that means "to cut" or "to separate." When the angels proclaim that God is holy, they are claiming that God is separate from anything or anyone else in creation. He is "a cut above" everyone and everything.

> *There really is only one word that can describe the totality of God's being:* holy.

When Isaiah saw the God Who Is (versus the God Isaiah may have imagined), the prophet was completely undone:

> Woe is me, for I am ruined!
> Because I am a man of unclean lips,
> And I live among a people of unclean lips;
> For my eyes have seen the King, the LORD of hosts.
>   (Isa. 6:5)

Author Mark Buchanan describes the experience of every person who is confronted with the holiness—the uniqueness—of the true God:

> Isaiah, though, can't join the song, not yet. His life is being re-defined for him. An encounter with God's holiness does that to us: It gives rise, not to song and dance, but to wild, harrowing terror. His holiness is heart-stopping, hair-raising. It scalds and rends and pierces. It elicits from our lips, our unclean lips, not "Wow!" but "Woe."

When we see God we also see ourselves. When we behold His holiness, we see in that instant our unholiness. His glory reveals our ruin, His purity our vanity, His light our shadows.... Before we can ever rest in the holiness of God, first we must be undone by it.[5]

God's holiness means that He is separate from everything— including sin. Unlike the gods of other religions who were imagined to participate in and thoroughly enjoy evil, the God revealed in the Old Testament is above and beyond any contact with evil. The prophet Habakkuk addressed God this way:

> Your eyes are too pure to approve evil,
> And You can not look on wickedness with favor.
> (Hab. 1:13)

Of all the attributes that create a distance between God and us, it is His zero tolerance for sin of any kind that makes Him "wholly different" from us. Sometimes we actually imagine ourselves to be morally superior to God because we are more accepting of sin than He is. For example, 2 Samuel 6 records the unusual experience of one of God's servants named Uzzah. The Israelites were transporting the ark of the covenant (which represented the holiness of God) up a steep hill on a cart. One of the oxen stumbled, and Uzzah instinctively reached out to steady the ark and keep it from falling off the cart.

You might assume that Uzzah's alertness and desire to protect such a sacred object would earn him a place in God's Hall of Fame. Wrong! Instead, his actions earned him a place in the cemetery:

> And the anger of the LORD burned against Uzzah, and God struck him down there for his irreverence; and he died there by the ark of God. (2 Sam. 6:7)

His "irreverence"? Wasn't it Uzzah's sincere reverence for God that caused him to reach out to protect the object associated with God's holiness?

The problem was that God had said no one was to touch the ark . . . period. But couldn't God overlook Uzzah's mistake and judge him by his motives? Why can't God be as tolerant of people's mistakes as we are? we

> *The fact that we can tolerate sin in others—and especially in ourselves—is not proof of our godliness but actually evidence of our ungodliness.*

wonder. Because God is not like us. The fact that we can tolerate sin in others—and especially in ourselves—is not proof of our godliness but actually evidence of our ungodliness.

God is wholly different than we are, which leads to a third theme revealed in the Old Testament.

The Sinfulness of Man

The holiness or separateness of God creates a moral distance between the Creator and us that began in the Garden of Eden and extends into our lives today. One writer vividly illustrates how our everyday choices illuminate the moral chasm between God and us:

A businessman on the road checks into a motel room late at night. He knows the kind of movies that are available to him in the room. No one will know. . . . First he has to say a little prayer: "Don't look at me, God."

A mom with an anger problem decides to berate her kids because she's so frustrated, because she will get a twisted rush of pleasure from inflicting pain. First she has to say a little prayer: "Don't look at me, God."

69

An executive who's going to pad an expense account—

An employee who is going to deliberately make a coworker look bad—

A student who looks at somebody else's paper during an exam—

A church member who looks forward to the chance to gossip—

First must say a little prayer.

We don't say it out loud, of course. We probably don't admit it even to ourselves. But it's the choice our heart makes:

Don't look at me, God.[6]

The first recorded instance in history of someone praying, "Don't look at me, God" is found in the Old Testament. God granted the First Couple freedom to enjoy the fruit of all the trees in the garden except one. Satan, utilizing a strategy he still finds successful today, drew Eve's attention away from God's innumerable gifts and caused her to fixate on God's single prohibition. "God is trying to keep you from enjoying the one experience that would really make you happy. The only reason He does not want you to eat from the forbidden tree is that He is afraid you will become like Him," the serpent claimed. He continues that refrain with us today.

"God is a cosmic killjoy who doesn't want you to have any fun."

"God is trying to prevent you from that one experience that will bring meaning into your life."

"God is paranoid that you will discover you really don't need Him."

Someone has said that all sin is rooted in contempt for God: God cannot be believed ("Has God said?" the serpent asked) or God cannot be trusted ("God knows that . . . you will be like

Him," the serpent charged). Unfortunately, Eve took the bait and the rest, as they say, is history:

> When the woman saw that the tree was good for food, and that it was a delight to the eyes, and that the tree was desirable to make one wise, she took from its fruit and ate; and she gave also to her husband with her, and he ate. (Gen. 3:6)

We might be tempted—so to speak—to think, *One little bite of forbidden fruit. What's the big deal? Everybody makes mistakes.* But this "mistake" resulted in seismic consequences for the entire human race, as the apostle Paul explains in Romans 5:12:

> Therefore, just as through one man sin entered into the world, and death through sin, and so death spread to all men, because all sinned.

Although Eve was certainly guilty of disobeying God, her disobedience can be traced to her deception by the serpent (Paul elaborates on this in 1 Tim. 2:14). But Adam's sin was rooted in deliberate defiance of the Creator's clear command—which explains why the condemnation of the entire race is traced to Adam and not Eve.

Paul describes this act of Adam's as the entry point of the sin virus that spread to the entire race. Because we are all descendants of the First Couple, we have all been infected with the destructive virus that separates us from God. We will let the theologians wrangle about what we actually inherit from Adam: his guilt, his predisposition to sin, or both. The fact is that every day of our lives we exercise the same defiance toward God and His commands that Adam did. As G. K. Chesterton observed, original sin is "the only part of Christian theology which can

71

really be proved."[7] If you don't believe that, just look around you
. . . or better yet, look inside you.

"Okay, I admit I occasionally make some mistakes, but I'm
not *that* bad!" some would protest. Recently, I had a biopsy
performed on a little polyp. I could have easily dismissed it and
said, "It's only a small polyp, and I feel fine. No big deal." But
such a diagnosis would have been meaningless because I'm not
a doctor and therefore not qualified to know the true state of
my health. Fortunately, the growth was benign.

Unfortunately, God has performed a biopsy of the human
condition and the results are not good. There is a malignancy
of the soul that leads to eternal death. It really doesn't matter
how any of us feels about the state of our spiritual health. The
only diagnosis that matters comes from the only One who can
truly see the condition of our heart. His "chart" contains these
descriptions of man's spiritual condition:

> Then the LORD saw that the wickedness of man was great on
> the earth, and that every intent of the thoughts of his heart was
> only evil continually. (Gen. 6:5)

> They are corrupt, they have committed abominable
>   deeds;
> There is no one who does good. . . .
> They have all turned aside, together they have become
>   corrupt;
> There is no one who does good, not even one.
>   (Ps. 14:1, 3)

> The heart is more deceitful than all else
> and is desperately sick;
> Who can understand it? (Jer. 17:9)

These Old Testament passages reveal a truth that theologians refer to as "the total depravity of man." This phrase describes the result of the sin we have inherited from Adam. Some people wince at the phrase *total depravity* not only because it is insulting to our sense of human dignity but also because it just doesn't seem true. After all, look at all the good things people of various faiths or no faith do: building homes for Habitat for Humanity, donating money to the poor, volunteering at hospice, or banding together to help victims of natural disasters. How can we honestly say those people are "totally depraved"?

The late Malcolm Muggeridge explained that belief in the total depravity of mankind does not mean we are all murderers, drug dealers, or sexual perverts:

> The truth is much deeper and more subtle than that. It is precisely when you consider the best in man that you see there is in each of us a hard core of pride or self-centeredness which corrupts our best achievements and blights our best experiences. It comes out in all sorts of ways—in jealousy which spoils our friendships, in the vanity we feel when we have done something pretty good, in the easy conversion of love into lust.[8]

The "total depravity of man" does not refer to the depth of our sinfulness but the breadth of our sinfulness. Our inherited sin nature has not pulled us as far down as we could possibly go (there's always room for more depravity), but it has spread and contaminated every aspect of our lives: our work, our family, our thoughts, and even our relationship with God.

When I was growing up, my father taught me how to make homemade ice cream. We would mix up the delicious recipe of eggs, cream, loads of sugar, and vanilla extract and place it in the steel container. We would then place that container in a large wooden bucket and pack the bucket with ice. A motor attached to the container would slowly turn it as the contents would harden into ice cream. During the churning of the container, I would place rock salt in the bucket to accelerate the melting of the ice. However, I dutifully and quickly brushed off any salt from the lid of the container. "It only takes one or two grains of salt to spoil the entire batch of ice cream," my dad would warn.

Once I was careless, thinking there was no way the salt could make it into the ice-cream container. I was wrong. When my family later sat down to partake of the frozen delight I had proudly created, they gagged in unison with the first bite. It only took a little salt to spoil an entire container of ice cream. Similarly, it only takes a little sin to contaminate an entire life.

The spiritual contamination that has infected all of us has created a spiritual chasm between God and us. We have difficulty grasping the vastness of that gulf because we use the wrong standard to assess our own spiritual condition. We tend to judge ourselves against other people (usually people we deem worse than we are). Compared to Adolph Hitler, Osama bin Laden, or the guy who deals drugs to children, we look pretty good.

Unfortunately, we are utilizing the wrong standard of measurement. Think of it this way. The geographical difference between the North Pole and the South Pole is great, but it is also negligible compared to the distance between the North Pole and the farthest star in the universe.

While we see a great deal of moral difference between a person like Walt Disney, who brought happiness to millions of children, and Adolph Hitler, who sent children to crematoriums by the trainload, those differences are negligible compared to the moral difference between us and a perfect God.

How can that chasm ever be bridged so that we can enjoy the same kind of relationship with God that Adam and Eve experienced prior to their disobedience? The answer to that dilemma is first discovered in the Old Testament, and it involves the fourth theme demonstrating the exclusivity of Christ for salvation.

The Need for Sacrifice

Immediately after Adam and Eve disobeyed God, they did something that may seem unusual:

> Then the eyes of both of them were opened, and they knew that they were naked; and they sewed fig leaves together and made themselves loin coverings. (Gen. 3:7)

Sin produces guilt, and guilt generates the need for a covering. Our natural instinct to try to cover up our mistakes rather than admit them is inherited from Adam and Eve. They instinctively thought the way to cover their sin was to cover up their mistake with garments of their own making.

But when God came looking for them "in the cool of the day" (Gen. 3:8) they must have felt a sudden draft as they realized how inadequate their self-manufactured apparel was in the presence of a holy God. Only when they grasped their inability to cover their very real guilt before God were they in a position to receive God's provision for their sin:

> The LORD God made garments of skin for Adam and his wife, and clothed them. (Gen. 3:21)

This verse records the very first death in the Bible. The skin for Adam's and Eve's covering came from an animal God had created and then killed to make a sufficient covering for His children's guilt. The first death in history was a sacrificial death. Something innocent died to cover the sins of someone guilty. And God was the One who provided the sacrificial animal.

Under Mosaic law, there were numerous and unending offerings and sacrifices God commanded as a perpetual reminder of the people's sins. The climactic offering for the sins of Israel as a whole occurred on the Day of Atonement, described in Leviticus 16.

Once a year, the Jewish high priest would enter into the most sacred place in the temple, the Holy of Holies, where God was thought to dwell. The Holy of Holies contained the ark of the covenant, a box that among other things contained the Ten Commandments given to Moses. On top of the box was a gold lid called the mercy seat. On each end of the box was the representation of a special kind of angel—a cherub associated with guarding the holiness of God.

The picture was clear. God, looking down at the ark of the covenant, saw His law being violated by His own people day after day. But once a year, the high priest—after offering a bull as a sacrifice for his own sin—would enter into the Holy of Holies and sprinkle the blood of a goat on the mercy seat, symbolically covering over (or atoning for) the sins of the people.

Thus, when God looked down at the ark, He no longer saw His law, which had been transgressed, but the blood of an animal covering the sins of the people. But who created the required sin offering? God reminded the Israelites that He was the One who created the animal they offered on the sacrificial altar:

> For the life of the flesh is in the blood, and I have given it to
> you on the altar to make atonement for your souls; for it is the
> blood by reason of the life that makes atonement. (Lev. 17:11)

Once again we see the picture of something innocent dying for those who are guilty.

One more example. In Genesis 22 we find the remarkable account of God commanding his servant Abraham to take his son Isaac to Mount Moriah and offer him has a burnt sacrifice. As Abraham raised his knife to plunge it into the heart of his beloved son, the Lord stopped him and instead provided a ram as a substitute for the sacrifice He had required. Moved with gratitude for what God had done, Abraham named the place Yahweh Yir'eh (meaning "The Lord Will Provide").

Nearly two thousand years later, in that same group of hills known as the region of Moriah, God would provide the ultimate sacrifice for the sins of mankind. It was in that same area many scholars believe that Jesus Christ, "the Lamb of God who takes away the sin of the world" (John 1:29), was crucified. Someone innocent died as a sacrifice for those of us who are guilty.

Every animal offered in the Old Testament sacrifices was required to be "without blemish." But these animals were simply an object lesson pointing to the ultimate sacrifice, Jesus Christ, whom God Himself would provide to atone for the sins of the world. Like the animal sacrifices, Jesus Christ was perfect. But that's where the similarity stops.

The Old Testament sacrifices had to be offered continually. Christ was offered once. The Old Testament sacrifices were made by sinful priests who had to atone for their own sins. Christ was the perfect High Priest who presented Himself as the sacrifice.

The Old Testament sacrifices provided temporary reconciliation with God. Christ's sacrifice offered eternal redemption for those who believe. The writer of Hebrews illustrates the contrast between the Old Testament sacrificial system and the sacrifice of Christ this way:

> But when Christ appeared as a high priest of the good things to come, He entered through the greater and more perfect tabernacle, not made with hands, that is to say, not of this creation; and not through the blood of goats and calves, but through His own blood, He entered the holy place once for all, having obtained eternal redemption. (Heb. 9:11–12)

My pastor, when I was growing up, used to say, "Your reaction to reading the book of Leviticus is a measure of your spirituality." If that's true, then I flunk the spirituality test! All of the specific instructions regarding offerings and sacrifices seem tedious to read. But I suppose that one "spiritual" response I have when reading Leviticus is gratitude to God for not requiring such complicated and continual rituals today.

The Old Testament sacrificial system was designed as a regular reminder of the very real problem of sin in each of us that must be atoned for.

The Old Testament sacrificial system was designed as a regular reminder of the very real problem of sin in each of us that must be atoned for. The fact that those sacrifices were never completed but had to be offered year after year created a longing for the once-for-all sin offering that only God Himself could make.

There is one final truth found in the Old Testament related to the issue of the exclusivity of salvation that is closely associated with the sacrificial system.

The Exclusivity of the Sacrifice

As you read through the Old Testament, one of the things you will notice is the specificity of God's instructions:

- When God commands Noah to build an ark, He gives Noah everything short of a set of blueprints regarding the size of the ark, the material to be used, the number of decks, and even the number of doors—one (Gen. 6:14–16).

- When God gives Moses instructions for the construction of the tabernacle, every detail of this portable worship center was included (Exod. 25–30), down to the intricate design of the garments worn by the priests who would represent the people to God (Exod. 28).

- When God gives the Israelites instructions about the offerings and sacrifices they were to offer, He never said, "Give whatever and however you feel led to give. I'm more interested in your heart than in the details." Instead, God clearly specified the exact requirements for the offerings, the sacrifices, and the one presenting those offerings and sacrifices (Lev. 16–27).

Here's the message that comes through loud and clear in the Old Testament: if you want to be in a right relationship with the one true God, whom you have alienated by your sin, then you must reconcile with Him on His terms, not yours. God is exclusive.

We see God's exclusivity illustrated in the story of Cain and Abel, two of Adam and Eve's many children (Gen. 5:4), who illustrate two very different approaches to reconciliation with God:

> So it came about in the course of time that Cain brought an offering to the LORD of the fruit of the ground. Abel, on his part also brought of the firstlings of his flock and of their fat portions. And the LORD had regard for Abel and for his offering; but for Cain and for his offering He had no regard. So Cain became very angry and his countenance fell. (Gen. 4:3–5)

Cain's anger led to the first murder (Gen. 4:8) and to the first lie to God recorded in the Bible (v. 9). But the obvious question this story raises is, "Why did God reject Cain's offering and accept Abel's?"

I've read numerous attempts to answer this question. Many people speculate that it was the attitude of each man's heart that resulted in God's approval or disapproval. Perhaps Abel joyfully offered his sacrifice while Cain begrudgingly brought his. But the passage never suggests that.

Some (especially us preacher types trying to encourage generous giving) will opine that Cain gave out of his surplus while Abel's offering represented a true sacrifice. Yet there is nothing in the text to indicate that either.

The reason Abel's offering was accepted and Cain's was rejected by God is no mystery but is plainly stated in Hebrews 11:4:

> By faith Abel offered to God a better sacrifice than Cain, through which he obtained the testimony that he was righteous, God testifying about his gifts, and through faith, though he is dead, he still speaks.

Many scholars agree that given God's penchant for exacting details, somewhere in the white space between Genesis 4:2 and 4:3 God gave Cain and Abel specific instructions regarding the kind of offering He desired: instructions that Abel followed, resulting in God's commendation, and that Cain rejected, resulting in God's condemnation.

God most likely asked both men for an animal sacrifice as another reminder of the seriousness of man's sin and the necessity for a blood offering to cover that sin—an offering that ultimately only God Himself could provide. Abel may not have understood the reasons for God's command, but that did not stop him from obeying.

However, Cain decided to ignore God's command and offer what he thought would be an equal, if not better, sacrifice. After all, wouldn't a beautifully displayed arrangement of fruit and grain on the altar be more aesthetically appealing than a bloody animal? Cain could take pride in that kind of offering . . . which is exactly why God did not ask for that kind of offering!

The sacrifice God demanded was not meant to communicate how like God they were (*Look at what God and I have done together*, Cain must have thought as he arranged the grapes and dates on the altar), but how unlike God they were—so sinful that the blood of an innocent animal was required to cover over their guilt.

Lest you think I'm reading too much into this story, the New Testament writer Jude asserts that Cain's act of disobedience was the genesis of every false religion in the world today:

Woe to them! For they have gone the way of Cain. (Jude 11)

"The way of Cain" refers to any individual who attempts to approach God on his or her own terms rather than on God's terms.

"The way of Cain" describes any religious system that attempts to earn God's favor by works and rituals rather than by reliance on God's grace.

"The way of Cain" is any religious system that appeals to our pride rather than our desperate condition before God.

"The way of Cain" emphasizes humanity's goodness rather than humanity's sinfulness.

"The way of Cain" says there are many paths that lead to God rather than one path.

"The way of Cain" leads to eternal death rather than eternal life: "There is a way which seems right to a man, but its end is the way of death" (Prov. 14:12).

Incidentally, these five key spiritual principles from the Old Testament—the oneness of God, the holiness of God, the sinfulness of man, the need for sacrifice, and the exclusivity of the sacrifice—constitute a clear and compelling way for us to share the message of the gospel from the pages of the Old Testament. This can be especially useful when discussing the need for salvation through Jesus Christ with someone of Jewish background or those who claim that Christianity is a "new" faith and is thus less credible than "older" religions.

Spiritual Laws about God

We tend to reject claims of exclusivity when it comes to spiritual issues because by definition spiritual issues deal with the unseen. Because no person has seen God, we assume that the spiritual laws and principles pertaining to God—such as how to approach God—are less exacting than, say, the laws of gravity and the physics that govern the visible world. But such an assumption can lead to catastrophe.

I will never forget August 2, 1985. In the early hours of that morning, I was landing at the Dallas–Fort Worth airport, preparing to go home and help my wife finish packing for our move later that afternoon to my first pastorate in Eastland, Texas. The pilot awakened me from my slumber with a weather report for the day that included thunderstorms in the late afternoon and early evening. *How inconvenient for a moving day*, I remember thinking. Not nearly as inconvenient as those thunderstorms would be to another group of passengers attempting to land later that day at the DFW airport on Delta Flight 191.

As Flight 191's captain, Ted Connors, prepared to land his jumbo jet at DFW that afternoon, he noticed a strange cloud formation at the end of runway 17L. At first he thought he might go around the cloud. But then he reasoned that he had hundreds of thousands of pounds of aircraft on his side, as well as three powerful Rolls-Royce engines and more than forty-three thousand hours of experience between his copilots. How much damage could a little wind and rain cause?

What Captain Connors, a highly competent and cautious pilot, did not realize was that in that cloud were powerful forces at work—wind shear, microbursts, and vortexes. As his plane made its way through the cloud, those invisible but real forces grabbed the jetliner and threw it against the ground, resulting in the loss of 137 lives.[9]

Just as there were natural laws of aerodynamics and physics that governed the invisible forces controlling that doomed plane, there are also spiritual laws that govern our approach to the invisible but very real God. We may think that we can alter those laws by approaching God in some other manner than His prescribed way, but when we do the result will be spiritual disaster.

These spiritual laws are communicated clearly throughout all the pages of the Bible—including both the Old Testament and the New Testament. Perhaps the clearest words of all about this subject are the ones that appear in red letters in your Bible— the words of Jesus Christ Himself. In the next chapter, we will discover what Jesus said about the issue of exclusivity and why His words matter to us today.

5

The Intolerant Christ

When you hear the name Jesus, what is the first word that comes to your mind? *Gentle, loving, patient,* and *compassionate* are usually the top choices. One descriptor that is usually not at the top of anyone's list is *intolerant.* To employ such a word to describe the Lamb of God borders on blasphemy, most people would think.

My college religion professor was teaching one day about the Israelites' victory at Jericho, during which "they utterly destroyed everything in the city, both man and woman, young and old, and ox and sheep and donkey, with the edge of the sword" (Josh. 6:21) according to God's prior instruction in Deuteronomy 20:16. God saw the Canaanites' idolatrous worship of many gods as a spiritual cancer that had to be eradicated from the land for the sake of the Israelites' spiritual health.

My college professor did not see it that way. "Do you really think God told Joshua to kill every man, woman, child, and animal living in Jericho? Of course not! Joshua simply imagined God said that because of his wrong image of God as a blood-thirsty warrior. Can you imagine Jesus of Nazareth ever doing such a thing?"

I raised my hand and replied, "I can!" The incredulous professor (who grew to really dislike me by the end of the semester) asked, "How can you say that?" I then referenced the verse about Christ's return to earth when He will slay the wicked (Rev. 19:15). The professor quickly dismissed that reference as "apocalyptic literature" that is not as "inspired" as the Gospel accounts of the meek and mild Teacher from Galilee. When I hear people trying to decide which portions of the Bible are truly inspired, I often think of what Dr. W. A. Criswell used to call "the leopard theory" of biblical inspiration: "The Bible is inspired in spots, and I'm inspired to spot the spots!"

But even the Gospel accounts of Jesus do not present Him as a one-dimensional, wimpy rabbi who roamed the countryside picking daisies, eating bird seed, and saying nice things to people. Author Dorothy Sayers contrasts this popular view of Jesus with the Jesus actually presented in the Gospels:

> The people who hanged Christ never, to do them justice, accused him of being a bore—on the contrary, they thought him too dynamic to be safe. It has been left for later generations to muffle up that shattering personality and surround him with an atmosphere of tedium. We have very efficiently pared the claws of the Lion of Judah, certified him "meek and mild" and recommended him as a fitting household pet for pale curates and pious old ladies. . . .
>
> We cannot blink at the fact that Jesus, meek and mild, was so stiff in his opinions and so inflammatory in his language that he

was thrown out of church, stoned, hunted from place to place, and finally gibbeted as a firebrand and a public danger. Whatever his peace was, it was not the peace of an amiable indifference.[1]

Someone has said, "When answering the question, 'What would Jesus do?' remember that turning over tables and chasing out the money changers with a whip is always within the range of options!" We need to be certain that our ideas about Jesus are based on reality as revealed in the Bible rather than on Sunday school stereotypes.

When it comes to the central issue of salvation, we must allow our beliefs to be shaped by what the founder of our faith, Jesus Christ, *actually* said, not by what we *wish* He had said. If you carefully and honestly search the Gospel accounts of Jesus's words (which are the only reliable repository we have for His teachings), you find that the real Jesus, versus the imaginary Jesus, drives a stake through universalism, pluralism, and inclusivism. As evidenced by His own words, Jesus clearly believes that a person can only be assured of going to heaven through exercising personal faith in Him.

> *When it comes to the central issue of salvation, we must allow our beliefs to be shaped by what the founder of our faith, Jesus Christ, actually said, not by what we wish He had said.*

What Jesus Taught about His Uniqueness

When Jesus walked the earth, gentiles (non-Jews) ruled the world. Gentiles, unlike the Jews, were known for their belief in a multitude of gods (polytheism). In the world in which Jesus ministered there were a number of religious cults, each with its own "savior" offering salvation. Those not attracted to those cults had the opportunity to worship one of the multitude of deities the Romans associated with their cities or trade guilds. In addition to the cults and Roman deities, one could choose to follow some of the exotic Eastern mystery religions that were taking root in Israel.

Against this polytheistic background, Jesus claimed to be much more than a good teacher, a worthy role model, or a revered prophet. Jesus claimed to be God—and just not any god. He claimed to be the one and only God first revealed in the Old Testament. This continual assertion by Jesus kept the Jewish leaders in a perpetual state of apoplexy and ultimately placed Him on a cross.

Perhaps you have heard the myth that Jesus never claimed to be God, but some overzealous followers concocted that fable hundreds of years later for political reasons (a popular belief among non-Christians as well as the basis for the bestselling book and movie *The Da Vinci Code*). Let me show you two instances in which Jesus plainly and forcefully declared that He is God.

John 8 records a long debate between the Pharisees and Jesus about the significance of the Old Testament patriarch Abraham. Abraham's importance to the Jews cannot be overstated. Abraham was to the Jews what George Washington is to Americans. He was the father of the Israelite nation. The Jews—especially the Pharisees—were convinced that all was right between them and God because they were physical descendants of Abraham.

But Jesus bursts their bubble by insisting that a person must be a spiritual descendant of Abraham by demonstrating the same obedience to God that Abraham did. "Surely You are not greater than our father Abraham, who died?" the Pharisees asked (John 8:53). Jesus's answer sent them reeling. "Your father Abraham rejoiced to see My day, and he saw it and was glad" (v. 56).

Now the Pharisees were sincerely confused. "Abraham has been dead for almost two thousand years, and you aren't even fifty years old. Yet you are claiming to have seen Abraham? How could that be?"

Jesus said to them, "Truly, truly I say to you, before Abraham was born, I am" (v. 58).

Jesus was not only claiming to have lived prior to Abraham—something remarkable in itself—but by using the phrase "I am" Jesus was making the ultimate declaration that He was in fact the God the Pharisees professed to love and worship.

The words *I Am* are a reference to the most holy name for God found in the Old Testament—a name so sacred that no Jew would ever utter it aloud. The Hebrew name is Yahweh, translated "I Am." It is the name God used to identify Himself to Moses when He appeared in the burning bush, commanding Moses to deliver the Israelites out of Egypt. "Exactly whom should I say told me all of this?" Moses wondered.

> God said to Moses, "I AM WHO I AM"; and He said, "Thus you shall say to the sons of Israel, '"I AM has sent me to you."'" (Exod. 3:14)

Jesus's use of "I am" to describe His relationship with Abraham was not lost on the Pharisees, as evidenced by their violent reaction:

> Therefore they picked up stones to throw at Him. (John 8:59)

With just two little words, Jesus was making the grandest pronouncement anyone could make about himself: "I am God."

Here's another example of Jesus claiming to be the one and only God of the Old Testament. Prior to His crucifixion Jesus endured a number of trials—more like kangaroo courts—before both Roman and Jewish authorities. Jesus's accusers falsely charged Him with threatening to tear down the temple. During one of those pseudotrials, the hour was late and the high priest Caiaphas was ready to go to bed, so he decided to cut to the chase with the bottom-line question:

Are you the Christ, the Son of the Blessed One? (Mark 14:61)

Jesus answered with those two words: "I am" (v. 62). He could have stopped there, but He didn't. To drive his point home (as well as drive His accusers crazy) He then quoted a passage from the book of Daniel:

And you shall see the Son of Man sitting at the right hand of Power, and coming with clouds of heaven. (Mark 14:62)

Jesus's quotation of Daniel 7:13 was about as subtle as a sledgehammer. The term "Son of Man" was a title used by Daniel to describe the Messiah who would one day rule over everything and everyone on earth:

> I kept looking in the night visions,
> And behold, with the clouds of heaven
> One like a Son of Man was coming,
> And He came up to the Ancient of Days [God the
>   Father]
> And was presented before Him.

And to Him was given dominion,
Glory and a kingdom,
That all the peoples, nations and men of every language
Might serve Him.
His dominion is an everlasting dominion
Which will not pass away;
And His kingdom is one
Which will not be destroyed. (Dan. 7:13–14)

By using this passage from Daniel to describe Himself, Jesus was saying to Caiaphas, "You had better enjoy sitting on your throne of power while you can, because one day you and I are going to switch places. Your authority is temporary, but My kingdom is forever."

If you think I'm reading too much into Jesus's words, notice how Caiaphas reacted to Jesus's declaration. He didn't turn to his advisers and ask, "What is all of this about 'Son of Man,' 'clouds,' and 'sitting at the right hand of power'?" Instead, when Jesus finished speaking . . .

Tearing his clothes, the high priest said, "What further need do we have of witnesses? You have heard the blasphemy; how does it seem to you?" And they all condemned Him to be deserving of death. (Mark 14:63–64)

I could devote the rest of the chapter to Jesus's other claims of deity, such as "I and the Father are one" (John 10:30) and "He who has seen Me has seen the Father" (14:9), but you get the idea.

Of course, anyone can claim to be God (though, interestingly, none of the other founders of major world religions such as

Buddha, Confucius, or Muhammad ever did). However, Jesus's uniqueness extended beyond who He claimed to be to what He claimed He could do:

- He could (and did) heal the sick (John 5:1–9).
- He could (and did) turn water into wine (John 2:1–11).
- He could (and did) raise the dead (John 11:43–44).
- He could (and did) calm the storms (Mark 4:35–41).
- He could (and did) forgive sins (Mark 2:1–12).

But by far the most unique claim Jesus ever made about Himself was that a person's eternal destiny depended upon his or her belief in Him:

> For this is the will of My Father, that everyone who beholds the Son and believes in Him will have eternal life; and I Myself will raise him up on the last day. (John 6:40)

Jesus does not offer eternal life to "everyone who is sincerely seeking truth" or to "everyone who believes in a god of his or her own choosing" or to "everyone who lives by a responsible moral code." According to Jesus, only someone who "believes in Him will have eternal life." This is why it is absolutely imperative that we share the message of the gospel with others. No matter how "good" or "moral" people may try to be, without Christ every single one of us will experience not eternal life but eternal death.

No other founder of a major religion ever linked someone's eternal well-being to his or her belief in that founder. But Jesus did. Even the Pharisees who worshiped the one true God, Yahweh, and attempted to follow His laws were not exempted from Jesus's condition for salvation:

Therefore I said to you that you will die in your sins; for unless you believe that I am He, you will die in your sins. (8:24)

But understanding Jesus's claims about Himself is just the first step to determining what He believed about the issue of exclusivity.

What Jesus Taught about His Death

It is impossible to overstate the positive impact of Jesus on the world in the last two thousand years both through His example and through His followers. For example, the concept of orphanages to care for parentless children and hospitals to care for the sick is rooted in Christianity. Swiss philanthropist Jean Henri Dunant started the International Committee of the Red Cross in the 1860s to minister in Jesus's name to soldiers dying on the battlefield.[2] The Salvation Army, whose mission is to "preach the gospel of Jesus Christ and to meet human needs in His name,"[3] distributes more than two billion dollars annually to those in need.[4]

The greatest educational institutions in our country, such as Harvard, Yale, William and Mary, and Princeton, were founded by Christ followers for the express purpose of educating students to know Jesus Christ. In fact, 92 percent of the first 138 colleges founded in America were begun by Christians.[5]

Christians—contrary to the claim of secularists—have advanced the study of science and technology. For example, Isaac Newton, Francis Bacon, Louis Pasteur, and Blaise Pascal were Christians who believed that the world was created by a God of order and could therefore be studied.

Contemporary historian Michael Grant summarizes the impact of Jesus's life and teachings this way:

> The most potent figure, not only in the history of religion, but in world history as a whole is Jesus Christ: the maker of one of the few revolutions which have lasted. Millions of men and women for century after century have found his life and teaching overwhelmingly significant and moving. And there is ample reason . . . in this later twentieth century why this should still be so.[6]

Jesus's "life and teaching" are certainly beyond compare, but they are also relatively insignificant when compared to the most important aspect of His life: His death. Contrary to popular belief, Jesus's crucifixion was not a tragic epilogue to an otherwise happy story, nor was His death a random and senseless act of violence that cut short a great life. Jesus's whole purpose in life was fulfilled by His death. Jesus was born to die.

Numerous times, Jesus told His followers and His detractors that His crucifixion was the means by which He would accomplish His mission on earth:

> From that time Jesus began to show His disciples that He must go to Jerusalem, and suffer many things from the elders and chief priests and scribes, and be killed, and be raised up on the third day. (Matt. 16:21)

> "And I, if I am lifted up from the earth, will draw all men to Myself." But He was saying this to indicate the kind of death by which He was to die. (John 12:32–33)

> Jesus said to them, "You will all fall away, because it is written, 'I will strike down the shepherd, and the sheep shall be scattered.'

But after I have been raised, I will go ahead of you to Galilee."
(Mark 14:27–28)

Jesus's life was not taken from Him prematurely or acciden-
tally. Repeatedly, Christ prophesied His impending death—a
sacrifice that He was voluntarily making:

> For this reason the Father loves Me, because I lay down My life
> so that I may take it again. No one has taken it away from Me,
> but I lay it down on My own initiative. I have authority to lay it
> down, and I have authority to take it up again. This command-
> ment I received from My Father. (John 10:17–18)

Why was Jesus's death central to His mission? Some believe
that Jesus's undeserved death gave mankind an example of how
to endure unjust suffering in life. Certainly the suffering of Christ
does provide us with a guide to responding when we are the
recipients of unfair accusations. The apostle Peter wrote:

> For you have been called for this purpose, since Christ also suf-
> fered for you, leaving you an example for you to follow in His
> steps . . . and while being reviled, He did not revile in return;
> while suffering, He uttered no threats, but kept entrusting Him-
> self to Him who judges righteously. (1 Pet. 2:21, 23)

What a great example for all of us who are on the receiving end
of abuse. No "give as good as you get" or vitriolic threats—just
saying, "God, I'm trusting You to make things right." Yet if that
is all Jesus's death accomplished, then there is nothing really
exclusive about it, since many men and women in history have
nobly endured mistreatment.

Jesus taught that the unique aspect of His death lay in what
the voluntary surrender of His life would accomplish:

The Son of Man did not come to be served, but to serve, and to give His life a ransom for many. (Matt. 20:28)

Jesus described His death as a ransom. The Greek word translated "ransom" referred to the price paid to purchase a slave. If someone needed a slave, he would travel to the marketplace and view a variety of men, women, and children in chains placed on the auction block. He could "redeem" (the word means to "take out of the marketplace") the slave by offering the required "ransom." The picture Jesus was painting could not be clearer.

All of us are born as slaves to sin and death, and Satan is our slave master. The "wages" he offers for our servitude to him are misery and death. But through Christ's sacrificial death, He has paid the necessary ransom to redeem us from our slavery to Satan and has freed us to serve God and enjoy the "wages" He offers. "The wages of sin is death, but the free gift of God is eternal life in Christ Jesus our Lord" (Rom. 6:23).

This new quality of life God offers that begins now and extends throughout eternity is "free" in the sense that it costs us nothing to receive, but it cost Christ everything to provide.

There is a story pastors often use to try to illustrate the extent of the sacrifice Christ made to pay this ransom. A nine-year-old girl was dying and desperately needed a blood transfusion. Because of her rare blood type and the urgency of the hour, the only one who could donate blood was her six-year-old brother. The parents explained the situation to the boy, and he agreed to donate his blood. After the transfusion was completed, the doctor patted the boy on the shoulder, complimenting him on his bravery. The little boy looked up at the physician and asked, "Doctor, how long before I die?" The boy mistakenly thought that transfusions resulted in death, yet he was willing to make the sacrifice if it would ensure his sister would live.

But here is where the illustration breaks down. It's one thing to sacrifice your life for a relative or someone else who loves you. But would you make that ultimate sacrifice for someone who hated you? That is what God did for us when He offered His Son, Jesus, as the ransom for our deliverance.

> For one will hardly die for a righteous man. . . . But God demonstrates His own love toward us, in that while we were yet sinners, Christ died for us. (Rom. 5:7–8)

As we have seen in previous chapters, the only reason Christ was willing to offer this ultimate sacrifice was because it was the only way to bridge the great gulf between God and man. "God and sinners reconciled," as the Christmas carol heralds.

Only when we appreciate the extent of Christ's physical—and more significantly His spiritual—agony on the cross as He paid the ransom for our sins can we understand why Jesus made this bold claim:

> I am the way, and the truth, and the life; no one comes to the Father but through Me. (John 14:6)

The context of this claim is crucial to understanding it. Jesus was preparing His disciples for His approaching death, resurrection, and ascension into heaven. He reassured them with the truth that even though He was temporarily leaving them, He would come back for them and take them to be with Him forever:

> In My Father's house are many dwelling places; if it were not so, I would have told you; for I go to prepare a place for you. If

97

I go and prepare a place for you, I will come again and receive you to Myself, that where I am, there you may be also. And you know the way where I am going. (vv. 2–4)

Thomas, one of the apostles, realized this was important information, so he wanted to be sure he understood what the Lord was saying. "We're not sure where You are going, so how are we supposed to know the way?" Thomas asked. Jesus would answer the "where" question soon when He would ascend into heaven in full view of all of His disciples (Acts 1:9–11). But Jesus could not allow the "How do we get there?" question to go unanswered. What is the way that leads to heaven?

I am the way, and the truth, and the life; no one comes to the Father but through Me. (John 14:6)

This is at the top of the list of difficult verses in the Bible—not because Jesus was unclear in what He was claiming but because He was all too clear. Jesus is not "a way" among many paths that lead a person to God. Nor is Jesus "the way" only for those who believe He is the way, like the Christian leader mentioned earlier who prayed, "And for those of us who are Christians, He is the Savior of the world." No, Jesus said He is the way for everyone. Jesus is the only gatekeeper to heaven. No one gets there without coming through Him. No matter how narrow-minded or intolerant this truth may seem to unbelievers, this is the substance of the gospel that God compels us to share with others.

Author William Beausay writes about a group of men who decided to go on a backcountry wilderness exploration trip in Canada. They arrived at the outfitter's camp on the edge of the woods and spent the morning preparing packs and supplies for the long journey. A member of the group noticed that the guide lacked maps for the wilderness region they would be exploring. And even worse than having no maps was that the guide had no compass either. The men approached the guide about their concern. He smiled and said, "Maps and compasses are not the way through these mountains. *I* am the way through the mountains."[7]

Jesus taught that His death bridged the chasm between God and us and that He alone can lead us safely through the wilderness of this world into the presence of God.

What Jesus Taught about Eternity

But what about those who fail to follow Jesus through the "valley of the shadow of death" (Ps. 23:4) and into the presence of God? Do they somehow end up at the same heavenly destination as those who do? If we are going to assess accurately what Jesus taught about the issue of exclusivity in salvation, then we have to examine carefully what He said about the issue of eternity.

First, Jesus taught that there are two distinct possibilities for people's eternal destination. Christ drove a stake through the universalist theory that all people, regardless of their faith, will end up in heaven. In His description of the judgments that will occur when He returns to earth, Jesus said:

> These will go away into eternal punishment, but the righteous into eternal life. (Matt. 25:46)

Jesus could have easily affirmed the universalists' position by saying, "Everyone, regardless of what he does or believes, will be granted eternal life." But He didn't. Instead, Jesus repeatedly warned that there is not one destination for all but rather two distinct roads in this life that lead to two very different destinations in the next life. When it comes to choosing a spiritual path, we must choose very carefully because our permanent, eternal destiny is at stake.

In Jesus's most extensive discourse about the afterlife, he related the story of a rich man and a poor man, Lazarus, who both died. Yet, even though they shared the same experience of death, they did not share the same destiny:

> Now the poor man died and was carried away by the angels to Abraham's bosom [a Jewish expression for the presence of God]; and the rich man also died and was buried. In Hades [the rich man] lifted up his eyes, being in torment, and saw Abraham far away and Lazarus in his bosom. And he cried out and said, "Father Abraham, have mercy on me, and send Lazarus so that he may dip the tip of his finger in water and cool off my tongue, for I am in agony in this flame." (Luke 16:22–24)

Second, in this story Jesus not only affirms that people face two possible eternal destinies when they die, but He also taught that one of those possibilities is hell. Of the 1,830 verses in the New Testament that contain Jesus's teachings, 13 percent of those verses deal with the subject of eternal judgment and hell. When you study those verses you will discover that Jesus believed hell is an actual location (Matt. 25:46), a place of physical suffering (Matt. 22:13; Luke 16:24), and, most devastatingly, an irrevocable destination (Luke 16:26).

Once a person dies and finds him- or herself in this place of eternal punishment, Jesus said, all opportunity for faith and repentance is over. In Jesus's story the rich man begged Abraham for relief from his suffering and, if that was not possible, for someone to leave heaven and warn his siblings on earth of the terrible destiny that awaited them. I imagine that this rich man, who had experienced the devastating reality of hell, would be the greatest evangelist of all time! But Abraham explained why it was impossible to grant his requests:

> And besides all this, between us and you there is a great chasm fixed, so that those who wish to come over from here to you may not be able, and that none may cross over from there to us. (v. 26)

Those who teach that hell—if it even exists—is only a temporary location, where occupants will have an opportunity to trust in Christ and experience deliverance from God's judgment, must completely dismiss Jesus's teaching that hell is a forever destination.

Finally, Jesus taught that the majority of humanity will occupy hell rather than heaven. One of the most frequently voiced objections to the exclusivity of Christ for salvation is the inevitable conclusion that only a few people will actually be saved. Just look at the numbers. Of the seven billion inhabitants on the earth, only two billion are labeled as Christians (mostly because of cultural factors rather than personal faith).[8] That means that if you believe that Christ offers the only path to heaven, you are saying that at least 75 percent of the earth's population is going to be condemned. Yet as disturbing as that conclusion is, it aligns perfectly with what Jesus taught about how small the population of heaven will be compared to the population of hell:

> Enter through the narrow gate; for the gate is wide and the way is broad that leads to destruction, and there are many who enter

through it. For the gate is small and the way is narrow that leads to life, and there are few who find it. (Matt. 7:13–14)

I realize that the concept of hell is offensive to most non-Christians, and even to many Christians. Theologian Clark Pinnock wrote:

> I consider the concept of hell as endless torment in body and mind an outrageous doctrine, a theological and moral enormity, a bad doctrine of the tradition which needs to be changed. How can Christians possibly project a deity of such cruelty and vindictiveness whose ways include inflicting everlasting torture upon His creatures, however sinful they may have been? Surely a God who would do such a thing is more nearly like Satan than like God.[9]

But those who object to the concept of an eternal and forever place of suffering that the majority of humanity will experience either unknowingly or conveniently overlook this one fact: most of what we know about hell comes from the lips of Jesus Christ Himself. As Dorothy Sayers observes:

> There seems to be a kind of conspiracy, especially among middle-aged writers of vaguely liberal tendency, to forget, or to conceal, where the doctrine of Hell comes from. . . . The doctrine of Hell is not "mediaeval": it is Christ's. It is not a device of "mediaeval priestcraft" for frightening people into giving money to the church: it is Christ's deliberate judgment on sin. . . . We cannot repudiate Hell without altogether repudiating Christ.[10]

Never forget, however, that the Jesus who taught about hell is the same Jesus who provided the way—the only way—to escape the horror of hell.

What Jesus Taught about the Necessity of Personal Faith

Repeatedly, Jesus rejected the claim of inclusivists that His sacrificial death provided salvation for everyone—believers and unbelievers alike. Instead, Jesus linked eternal life to personal belief:

> Truly, truly, I say to you, he who hears My word, and believes Him who sent Me, has eternal life, and does not come into judgment, but has passed out of death into life. (John 5:24)

> For this is the will of My Father, that everyone who beholds the Son and believes in Him will have eternal life, and I Myself will raise him up on the last day. (6:40)

> Jesus said to her, "I am the resurrection and the life; he who believes in Me will live even if he dies, and everyone who lives and believes in Me will never die. Do you believe this?" (11:25–26)

When missionary John Paxton landed in the New Hebrides in the 1800s, he immediately began working on a translation of the New Testament the residents could understand. However, when he came to the word *believe* he was perplexed by how to illustrate the concept in an intelligible way. One day he leaned on a chair in such a way that his entire weight was resting on the chair, and he realized that is the true concept of *believe*—to place your entire weight upon something.

Many years ago, I decided to use that illustration in a sermon in the first church I pastored. I stood by one of the massive chairs behind the pulpit and said, "I can say that I believe this chair will support me, but until I put my whole weight in this chair it will not actually support me." I then began to sit lightly in the chair but kept the bulk of my weight on my feet. "Is this chair supporting me?" "No," the congregation shouted back in unison. Finally, I sat down in the chair with my entire weight supported by the chair. "Only when I believe enough to place my entire weight on the chair do I truly believe in the chair's ability to support me."

As I was speaking I began to hear a cracking sound and suddenly the chair collapsed, unceremoniously dumping me on the ground. I've never heard a congregation laugh so hard or for so long. Finally, I made a subsidiary point: "But faith is only as good as the object of your faith!" When Jesus spoke about the necessity of faith for salvation it was not faith in anything or faith in faith, it was faith "in Me."

Since Jesus claimed eternal salvation only belongs to those who believe in Him, it is critical that we understand what Jesus had in mind when He talked about belief. Jesus was not saying that we need to believe in Him the same way we believe in a historical figure like Abraham Lincoln.

Many people erroneously equate belief with intellectual assent to a certain body of facts: Jesus was the Son of God who died on a cross for the sins of the world and rose from the dead on the third day. A person can believe in all those facts and still not receive eternal life. In fact, as you read the New Testament you will discover that some of the greatest professions about Jesus being the Messiah came from the lips of demons who immediately recognized Him as the Son of God (Matt. 8:29; Luke 4:41).

Satan and his minions fully believe that Jesus is the Son of God. They believe that Jesus died for the sins of the world (which is why they tried to destroy His life prematurely before He could accomplish His mission). And yes, they believe that He rose again from the dead. In fact, they believe all those facts about Jesus more than we do—because they were eyewitnesses to those events! But no one expects to see Satan and his demons in heaven because of their belief in the facts about Jesus.

Jesus equated belief with "trusting in, clinging to, resting in" His sacrificial death for salvation. How do I know that? Consider Jesus's explanation and illustration of believing that He gave to a man named Nicodemus.

If any man were a candidate for salvation apart from personal faith in Jesus it would have been Nicodemus. John describes him as "a man of the Pharisees" and "a ruler of the Jews" (John 3:1). Many Christians have the wrong idea about Pharisees, equating their moral character with that of used car salesmen or televangelists. In truth, the Pharisees were committed to showing their sincere love for God by trying as hard as they could to observe every part of the Mosaic law. Additionally, as "a ruler of the Jews," Nicodemus was part of the elite group known as the Sanhedrin—a group of approximately seventy Jewish men who were charged with deciding the most complex issues among the Jewish people.

If any person was able to qualify for heaven by his sincere love for God and his careful observance of God's laws, it should have been Nicodemus. Yet Jesus said to Nicodemus, "You must be born again" (v. 7). Remember, Jesus was not speaking to a drug dealer, child molester, or worshiper of pagan deities. Instead, Jesus said that even a leader of God's chosen nation, Israel, still needed to place complete faith in Him to obtain eternal life.

To illustrate what saving faith is, Jesus used a story from the Old Testament with which a faithful Jew like Nicodemus would have been very familiar:

> And as Moses lifted up the serpent in the wilderness, even so must the Son of Man be lifted up; so that whoever *believes* will in Him have eternal life.
>
> For God so loved the world, that He gave His only begotten Son, that whoever *believes* in Him shall not perish, but have eternal life. (vv. 14–16)

The story Jesus is alluding to is found in Numbers 21. Because of the Israelites' continued rebellion and ingratitude, God sent poisonous snakes to bite them. As they watched many of their fellow Israelites die, the people begged Moses to ask God to heal those who had been bitten by the serpents.

So God instructed Moses to make a bronze image of a serpent, place it on a pole, and tell the people that if anyone who had been bitten by a serpent would look up at the bronze image on a pole he would immediately be healed and would live:

> And Moses made a bronze serpent and set it on the standard; and it came about, that if a serpent bit any man, when he looked to the bronze serpent, he lived. (Num. 21:9)

God could have certainly provided healing for every Israelite who was dying—but He didn't. Instead, God's healing was restricted to those who demonstrated their faith in God's ability to deliver them from death by looking one time at the serpent on the pole.

I think it is very significant that of all the illustrations Jesus could have used to explain how a person can be saved from eternal death, He chose this one:

As Moses lifted up the serpent in the wilderness, even so must the Son of Man be lifted up; so that whoever believes will in Him have eternal life. (John 3:14–15)

In the verse that follows, Jesus applies that story to the issue of salvation:

For God so loved the world, that He gave His only begotten Son, that whoever believes in Him shall not perish, but have eternal life. (v. 16)

Eternal life is given only to those who exercise faith in His ability to deliver them from the eternal consequences of sin. For the Israelites, a one-time glance at the bronze serpent brought healing. For us today, a one time belief in Jesus's ability to forgive our sins brings eternal life. It really doesn't matter how much or how little faith we have. It's not the amount of faith that saves us but the object of our faith that saves us.

Pastor Charles Stanley illustrates that truth in this way. Imagine that you see an apartment building on fire and a crowd of people shouting and pointing to a woman trapped on the ledge of the third floor. She is understandably frightened and confused. Fortunately, the firefighters are holding a net below her and they encourage her to jump. The woman leaps from the burning building and lands safely in the net without any injury.

What saved the woman's life? Obviously, it was the net. No one would say the woman saved her own life. Instead, the firefighters saw the woman's need, formulated a plan for her deliverance, and executed the plan. All the woman had to do was to have enough faith in the net to take that leap.[11]

It's important to note that it wasn't the woman's action of jumping that saved her. On September 11, 2001, we saw the horrific scene of dozens of people leaping from the World Trade Center, resulting in their deaths because there was no net below capable of saving them. It was the net that spared the woman. Her leap of faith simply bridged the gap between her need and the provision waiting below.

The same is true of faith in Christ. No one is saved by his or her faith. Instead, Jesus taught that our faith is what bridges the gap between our desperate need for God's forgiveness and His provision for our need. Only those who look to Christ for salvation shall live. This is the urgent message we should be boldly and clearly sharing with others.

Jesus taught that our faith is what bridges the gap between our desperate need for God's forgiveness and His provision for our need.

Jesus's teaching that only those who exercise faith in Him will be saved should settle the matter. Nevertheless, as we will see in the next chapter, the exclusivity of the gospel is a consistent theme throughout the entire New Testament, beginning with the teaching of the first leader of the Christian church.

6

Why New Testament Jews Were for Jesus

When my daughter Julia was eleven, she begged me to take her to see the blockbuster movie *Titanic*. To this day my wife has not forgiven me for allowing our now-grown daughter to be exposed to the steamy love scene between Leonardo DiCaprio (who was the reason for my daughter's interest in the film) and Kate Winslet. But the movie did have some redeeming historical value as it recounted one of the greatest disasters in the twentieth century, in which more than fifteen hundred people lost their lives.

However, the screenwriter omitted one of the most dramatic scenes of the *Titanic* story that occurred in the days following its sinking. As the news of the ship's fate spread throughout the world, the officials from the White Star Line had to determine how to inform relatives whether their loved ones had survived or perished. Accordingly, outside the White Star office in Liverpool, England, the company set up a large sign that was divided into two columns. The heading on the left side read, "Known to Be Saved" and the heading on the right side read, "Known to Be Lost."

As the messenger would emerge from the office with the name of another passenger, the assembled crowd would wait anxiously to see on which side the name would be listed. While onboard the ship the passengers had experienced a variety of different categories of service—first class, second class, third class, and steerage. But after the sinking, passengers were placed in one of only two categories: saved or lost.[1]

The same is true of everyone who lives and dies. While there is great economic, geographic, religious, and ethnic diversity among the seven billion residents of planet Earth, when we die there are only two designations that matter: saved or lost. As we saw in the previous chapter, Jesus Christ affirmed that there are only two roads in life, which lead to two different destinies:

> Enter through the narrow gate; for the gate is wide and the way is broad that leads to destruction, and there are many who enter through it. For the gate is small and the way is narrow that leads to life, and there are few who find it. (Matt. 7:13–14)

The road that leads to destruction is deceptive because it is so wide and has so many people traveling on it. "How could so many people be wrong?" ask people who struggle with the idea of Christ offering the only way to heaven. After all, the vast majority of the world's population are not Christian. All the people who are on this "highway to hell"—including Buddhists, Hindus, Jews, Protestants, Catholics, and atheists—share one characteristic: although they may have embraced different lies, they have rejected the same truth.

What is that truth? It is that narrow belief that faith in Jesus is the only way a person can enter into heaven. And just in case anyone was confused about what that narrow gate is, Jesus said, "I am the way, and the truth, and the life; no one comes to the Father but through Me" (John 14:6).

When I was six years old the first Six Flags amusement park opened in the Dallas–Fort Worth metroplex, where I lived. As a child and later as a teenager I recall the throngs of people assembling in a plaza outside the park every summer day, waiting for the park to open. When that moment came, everyone would rush toward the entrance wanting to get in as quickly as possible. But the process was slowed down because everyone had to go one-by-one through a turnstile.

Jesus taught that the way to heaven is narrow like a turnstile. No one travels into heaven as part of a group but rather we enter one at a time through our faith in Jesus. As we saw in the previous chapter, Jesus clearly slammed the door on the idea that there are multiple paths that lead to heaven . . . or did He?

We should not be surprised when secularists or adherents of non-Christian religions embrace the idea that all religions lead to heaven. But what about Christian leaders who also teach—or leave the door slightly ajar to—the possibility that there may be another way into heaven other than faith in Christ? For example, consider the words of the late Pope John Paul II:

> Those who have chosen the way of the Gospel Beatitudes and live as "the poor in spirit," detached from material goods, in order to raise up the lowly of the earth from the dust of their

humiliation, will enter the kingdom of God. . . . All the just of the earth, including those who do not know Christ and his Church, who, under the influence of grace, seek God with a sincere heart . . . are thus called to build the kingdom of God.[2]

Fr. Richard Rohr, a Franciscan priest, is a popular Catholic author and founder of the Center for Action and Contemplation. In his recent book, *Eager to Love*, he writes of the "inclusivity" he sees in the gospel:

There is a universal accessibility, invitation, and inclusivity in an authentic Franciscan spirituality. It surpasses the boundaries of religion, culture, gender, ethnicity, era, class, or any measure of worthiness or education.[3]

Similarly, esteemed Catholic author Henri Nouwen wrote:

I personally believe that while Jesus came to open the door to God's house, all human beings can walk through that door, whether they know about Jesus or not. Today I see it as my call to help every person claim his or her own way to God.[4]

It is not just respected Catholics who reject the idea of exclusivity. The late Dr. Robert Schuller, founder of the Crystal Cathedral and former host of *The Hour of Power*, said in an interview:

Is there any possibility of a person being, quote—saved— unquote, without accepting Jesus Christ in a way evangelicals preach it today? My answer is, I don't know. That's the honest to God truth. But I believe in the sovereignty of God and the sovereignty of Jesus Christ. I hope so. Is it possible to be saved without making public repentance? I think so. On the cross, Jesus said, "Father, forgive them for they know not what they do." He didn't say, "Father, forgive them because they repented." Jesus has a different theology of salvation than most preachers.[5]

Brian McLaren is another Christian leader and thinker who teaches that the door to heaven is open to religions other than Christianity. Hailed by *Time* magazine as one of "The 25 Most Influential Evangelicals in America,"[6] McLaren is a leader in the emerging church movement and popular among younger Christians. He writes:

> Is our religion the only one that understands the true meaning of life? Or does God place his truth in others too? . . . The gospel is not our gospel, but the gospel of the kingdom of God, and what belongs to the kingdom of God cannot be hijacked by Christianity. . . . To put it in different terms, there is no salvation outside of Christ, but there is salvation outside of Christianity.[7]

The late Dallas Willard, well-known Southern Baptist author and professor at the University of Southern California, said in an interview with *Cutting Edge* magazine:

> I am not going to stand in the way of anyone whom God wants to save. I am not going to say "he can't save them." I am happy for God to save anyone he wants in any way he can. It is possible for someone who does not know Jesus to be saved.[8]

Now to be fair to the religious leaders I just quoted, some might argue that they were referring to people who have never heard of Jesus Christ. Is it possible that those who have never had the opportunity to hear about Jesus Christ will somehow be saved? Is it fair that God would condemn people to hell for rejecting a message they had never heard?

Since we are going to explore that issue in the next chapter, we will exclude those who have never heard the gospel from our discussion for now. Instead, let's focus on those who have heard the gospel of Jesus Christ but have rejected it. Does the Bible offer any alternative path that leads to heaven?

> *Why would Jesus go through the physical horror of crucifixion and, more significantly, the spiritual agony of separation from God if there were another way by which humanity could be reconciled to God?*

As we have seen, Jesus answered that question with a resounding "no" both through His words in John 14:6 ("no one comes to the Father but through Me") and through His experience on the cross. Why would Jesus go through the physical horror of crucifixion and, more significantly, the spiritual agony of separation from God if there were another way by which humanity could be reconciled to God?

But perhaps we are being too narrow-minded about this. Is it possible that we have misinterpreted Jesus's beliefs on this issue? Could we be reading into Jesus's words a message of exclusivity that He never intended? These are the questions that many unbelievers—and even some Christians—who struggle with the issue of exclusivity are asking today. How should we respond?

All one has to do is to read past the Gospels to discover that the consistent message of the entire New Testament is that personal faith in Christ is the only means by which a person can be saved.

Red Letters versus Read Letters

A few years ago when I appeared on Bill Maher's HBO program *Real Time*, Maher asked me about capital punishment in light of Jesus's words that condemn seeking personal vengeance against those who wrong you. I pointed out that in Romans 13:4 God grants government the power to "bear the sword" to execute justice against evildoers. "But Paul wrote that, not Jesus," Maher protested. "Yes, but Paul's words in the Bible were just as inspired as Jesus's words," I countered. "Whaaaaaaaat?" Bill shrieked in a falsetto voice as the audience roared with laughter. "That's right, Bill. Remember both Jesus's and Paul's words are all found in the same book," I explained.[9]

Bill Maher is not unique. Many people—including Christians—mistakenly believe that only the red-letter words in the New Testament are inspired because they represent the words of Jesus. They assume the words of Paul, Peter, and the other New Testament writers are not as authoritative as the words spoken by Jesus.

But historic Christianity has taught that all of the New Testament is equally *inspired* (a word meaning "God-breathed") and is just as authoritative as the Old Testament *Scriptures* (a word meaning "writings"). For example, Paul equates the authority of Moses's words in Deuteronomy with Luke's Gospel in the New Testament (1 Tim. 5:18). Peter, who had his share of disagreements with Paul, still categorizes Paul's writings as Scripture (2 Pet. 3:15–16).

Therefore, when examining this issue of the exclusivity of Christ we need to understand not only what Jesus believed about the issue but also what the writers of the New Testament had to say. And not surprisingly, their message is consistent with the words of Jesus: there is no other way to heaven except through faith in Christ alone.

The Teaching of the Apostle Peter

Pope Francis raised more than a few eyebrows when he declared, "The Lord has redeemed all of us, all of us, with the Blood of Christ: all of us, not just Catholics. Everyone! 'Father, the atheists?' Even the atheists. Everyone!"[10] Is it true that everyone will be redeemed—even atheists—regardless of what they believe?

Perhaps it would be helpful to look back and see what the apostle Peter—the man Catholics believe was the first pope—had to say about the subject. Regardless of whether you believe Peter was the first pope, he was the undisputed leader of the other apostles and the church at Jerusalem. As part of the inner circle of Jesus's closest associates, he was in a position to know Jesus's beliefs as well as anyone. What did Peter have to say about the issue of exclusivity?

Just weeks after Jesus's death and resurrection, thousands of Jews from all over Israel traveled to Jerusalem for the feast called Pentecost. Most of these Israelites had been in Jerusalem weeks earlier for the celebration of Passover, when Christ was crucified, and news of His subsequent resurrection had spread like wildfire.

As thousands of these same Israelites again gathered in Jerusalem for another feast, Peter stood on the southern steps of the temple and addressed the assembled crowd—many of whom weeks earlier had demanded that Pilate crucify Christ:

> Men of Israel, listen to these words: Jesus the Nazarene, a man attested to you by God with miracles and wonders and signs

which God performed through Him in your midst, just as you yourselves know—this Man, delivered over by the predetermined plan and foreknowledge of God, you nailed to a cross by the hands of godless men and put Him to death. But God raised Him up again. . . . Therefore let all the house of Israel know for certain that God has made Him both Lord and Christ—this Jesus whom you crucified. (Acts 2:22–24, 36)

Peter's accusatory words could have incited the crowd to riot. Instead, Luke records, "When they heard this, they were pierced to the heart, and said to Peter and the rest of the apostles, 'Brethren, what shall we do?'" (v. 37).

Do? Why would members of the "house of Israel" need to do anything? After all, they were already part of God's chosen nation. The males would have been circumcised. They regularly offered sacrifices as the Old Testament prescribed. Was Peter implying that their sincerely held Jewish beliefs were not enough? Apparently so, as evidenced by his response to their question:

Peter said to them, "Repent, and each of you be baptized in the name of Jesus Christ for the forgiveness of your sins; and you will receive the gift of the Holy Spirit." (v. 38)

Don't miss the significance of the fact that the first sermon ever preached after Christ's resurrection was delivered by a Jew (Peter) to a Jewish audience. And the heart of the message was that everyone—Jews included—must trust in Jesus Christ for the forgiveness of sins.

We see Peter's insistence concerning Christ's exclusivity again just a few chapters later in Acts 4. Peter and the other apostles were arrested by the Jewish authorities for continuing to preach the message of Christ's resurrection and to heal people by invoking the name of Jesus Christ. Luke records that more than five thousand Israelites had already turned to faith in Christ (v. 4). Feeling the increasing pressure to stop what they viewed as a growing heresy, the Jewish leaders demanded to know "in what name" the apostles were preaching and healing (v. 7).

Fortunately, Peter was not infected with political correctness like many Christians today who refuse to invoke the name of Jesus if it offends others. Instead, Peter answered confidently:

> Let it be known to all of you and to all the people of Israel, that by the name of Jesus Christ the Nazarene, whom you crucified, whom God raised from the dead—by this name this man stands here before you in good health. . . . And there is salvation in no one else; for there is no other name under heaven that has been given among men, by which we must be saved. (vv. 10, 12)

It is popular today for inclusivists to argue that people of various religious faiths are all worshiping the same God, even though they call Him by different names. It's highly likely that you have encountered this viewpoint as you are sharing the gospel or discussing matters of faith. One poll revealed that an astounding 63 percent of Americans say Christians, Jews, Muslims, and Buddhists all "pray to the same God," although they call him by different names.[11]

Yet our attempt to minimize the importance of a name is disingenuous. For example, if you are applying for a car loan and your name is Cindy Jones, imagine what would happen if you signed the loan document as Janet Smith? When challenged by the loan officer about your signature, could you get away by saying, "Oh, that's just another name I sometimes use to refer to myself"? Of course not! Your name is important because it represents who you are. When other people hear your name, they think of your appearance, your voice, your character qualities, and your actions.

When Peter declared there is "no other name . . . by which we must be saved" (v. 12), he forever closed the door on the mistaken concept that other religions worship the same Jesus but call Him by a different name. Regardless of how the name "Jesus Christ" is translated in various languages, it is still a reference to the Jesus whose life and attributes are described in the Bible, not the gods of other religions recorded in books of spiritual mythology.

Peter and Cornelius

One of the clearest arguments for the necessity of personal faith in Christ for salvation is found in Peter's role in the conversion of the Roman centurion named Cornelius:

> Now there was a man at Caesarea named Cornelius, a centurion of what was called the Italian cohort, a devout man and one who feared God with all his household, and gave many alms to the Jewish people and prayed to God continually. (Acts 10:1–2)

Although Cornelius was a gentile, this Roman soldier worshiped the God of the Jews, as evidenced by his gifts to the Jewish people. Stop and consider this for a moment. If you asked the average person on the street if someone who believed in God, prayed regularly, and gave money to the poor would be welcomed into heaven when he died, the overwhelming majority of people would answer, "Without a doubt!"

Yet Cornelius's sincere faith in the one true God, coupled with his righteous actions, was not enough to secure his eternal salvation. As we read through the rest of Acts 10 we discover how God supernaturally orchestrated events to bring the apostle Peter to Cornelius so that Cornelius, along with his family and closest friends, could hear and personally embrace the gospel of Jesus Christ.

When Peter stood before Cornelius, he didn't say, "Cornelius, I can tell that you are a righteous man who loves God. You don't need to do anything else. Just 'keep on keeping on!'" Not on your life. Instead, Peter began to share with Cornelius and the group the truth about Jesus's death and resurrection. Then the apostle closed with these words:

> And [God] ordered us to preach to the people, and solemnly to testify that this is the One who has been appointed by God as Judge of the living and the dead. Of Him all the prophets bear witness that *through His name everyone who believes in Him receives forgiveness of sins.* (vv. 42–43)

Luke records that Cornelius and his group immediately believed Peter's message about Christ as evidenced by their baptism both by water and with the Holy Spirit of God (vv. 44–48).

This incident from the ministry of Peter should forever drive a stake through the inclusivists' argument that a person who loves God can be saved by Jesus Christ without ever personally trusting in Christ for salvation.

Admittedly, the inclusivist position is appealing because it offers the hope of salvation to billions of religious people who are otherwise condemned to hell. Theologian Peter Kreeft asks, "When a pious Muslim practices Islam, his submission, might this be taking place through Christ and his grace and presence, though the Muslim does not know it or acknowledge it? I think this is very likely."[12]

Let's substitute the Roman centurion Cornelius (Acts 10) for Kreeft's hypothetical Muslim. When a pious gentile like Cornelius practices Judaism, could his worship be taking place through Christ even though Cornelius does not know it or acknowledge it? In other words, is Cornelius in a right relationship with God even though he has never trusted in Jesus Christ? If the answer is yes, then Peter made a wasted trip to Caesarea to preach to Cornelius, along with his family and friends. In fact, if inclusivism were true and Cornelius was already in a right relationship with God without personal faith, then Peter's sermon to Cornelius would have been offensive because it was based on the false presupposition that Cornelius's religious beliefs were inferior to Peter's.

But both Cornelius and Peter demonstrated by their words and actions that in fact Cornelius's faith in God and his righteous actions were not sufficient for him to secure eternal life. Cornelius needed something more—and that something more was the gospel of Jesus Christ.

The Apostle Paul

One of the "gotcha" questions the media loves to ask evangelical pastors is, "Do you believe a Jewish person who sincerely practices his religion without accepting Christ is going to hell?" I've seen pastors begin to sweat, stutter, and then sputter out something like, "Only God can make that judgment."

Whenever I'm asked that question, I respond with a simple, "Yes. It doesn't matter whether you are Jewish, Muslim, Catholic, or Baptist, you can't go to heaven without faith in Jesus Christ as your Savior." I then remind the interviewer that the three most prominent Jews in the New Testament—Jesus, the apostle Peter, and the apostle Paul—believed and taught that message of exclusivity as well.

The Experience of Paul

If anyone should have been able to enter heaven on the basis of his religious credentials, it should have been the apostle Paul. He recounts his spiritual pedigree prior to his conversion this way:

> Circumcised the eighth day, of the nation of Israel, of the tribe of Benjamin, a Hebrew of Hebrews; as to the Law, a Pharisee; as to zeal, a persecutor of the church; as to righteousness which is in the Law, found blameless. (Phil. 3:5–6)

Translation: "I was a pure-blooded Israelite who sincerely followed the teachings of my Jewish faith to the letter of the law." In fact, Paul was so committed to his belief system that he did everything he could to stamp out what he considered to be the growing heresy of Christianity. Paul's persecution of Christians prior to his conversion was not rooted in sadism but in the sincerity of his faith.

But on his way to torture, imprison, and murder followers of Christ in Damascus, Paul had an encounter with Jesus Christ that forever changed the course of his life and of history:

> As he was traveling, it happened that he was approaching Damascus, and suddenly a light from heaven flashed around him; and he fell to the ground and heard a voice saying to him, "Saul,

Saul [Paul's Jewish name], why are you persecuting Me?" And he said, "Who are You, Lord?" And He said, "I am Jesus whom you are persecuting." (Acts 9:3–5)

That confrontation with Jesus Christ transformed Paul from the greatest antagonist to the greatest evangelist for the Christian message.

Paul's Ministry of Exclusivity

Paul was unlike many Christians today who acknowledge Christ as their own Savior but are hesitant to insist that He is the only possible Savior for everyone else. Not Paul. In the prologue of his letter to the Christians in Rome, Paul declared:

> I am not ashamed of the gospel, for it is the power of God for salvation to everyone who believes, to the Jew first and also to the Greek. (Rom. 1:16)

At first glance, Paul's declaration seems strange. "Not ashamed of the gospel"? Why would anyone ever feel that way about the Christian message? Yet when we are honest, there are times when those of us who are Christians signal our embarrassment of the gospel:

- when we fail to speak up in class while a teacher is ridiculing the basic tenets of the Christian faith.
- when we are fearful of sharing the gospel message with a family member who is an unbeliever.
- when we are hesitant to share the message of Christ with the follower of another religion for fear of offending him or her.

123

- when we are reluctant to insist too strongly with an intellectual friend that Christ offers the only way to heaven.

Paul never backed down from proclaiming the exclusivity of Christ, regardless of what happened to him as a result:

Five times I received from the Jews thirty-nine lashes. Three times I was beaten with rods, once I was stoned, three times I was shipwrecked, a night and a day I have spent in the deep. . . . I have been in labor and hardship, through many sleepless nights, in hunger and thirst, often without food, in cold and exposure. (2 Cor. 11:24–25, 27)

Now here is a simple question: If everyone is going to heaven regardless of his beliefs or if there are multiple routes that lead to the same destination of heaven, then why did Paul endure all that suffering (including his own death) to preach the message of Jesus Christ? Paul believed that only the gospel of Jesus Christ provided "salvation to everyone who believes" (Rom. 1:16).

Paul uses the term *salvation* or *save* thirteen times in his letter to the Romans. Here, he links the word *salvation* with the word *gospel* (meaning "good news"). The message that Jesus Christ died for our sins is "good news" because it is God's means of rescuing us from an eternity of separation from God.

Several years ago the awarding-winning movie *Gravity* told the story of two astronauts stranded in space looking for a way back home. Any plan of action that would deliver them safely home was not bad news; it would have been good news. No matter how "exclusive" that plan might be, if it could rescue both of them from their fate and bring them safely home, then it would have been the most loving thing for anyone to share.

The Bible teaches that all of mankind is hopelessly adrift as we move further and further away from God. Isaiah the prophet said it this way:

> All of us like sheep have gone astray,
> Each of us has turned to his own way. (Isa. 53:6)

But instead of allowing us to experience the deserved consequences of our spiritual departure from our Creator, God formulated a rescue plan to bring us back to Him—and that plan for our salvation is the gospel of Jesus Christ.

The Teaching of Paul

Paul did not subscribe to the inclusivist view that God's plan resulted in the rescue of everyone. Paul did not write, "I am not ashamed of the gospel, for it is the power of God for salvation to everyone." Instead, Paul uses two words that restrict the scope of those God saves: "to everyone *who believes*."

Just as

- a tether in outer space can only save the astronaut who takes hold if it,
- a net can only save from a burning building the woman who is willing to jump into it, and
- a life preserver can only save the drowning person who grabs on to it,

so the gospel of Jesus Christ can only save those who believe in it. Like Jesus, the apostle Paul never separated salvation from personal faith. So that his readers did not miss that point, in the very next verse Paul explains that faith is an essential ingredient of the gospel:

> For in it [the gospel] the righteousness of God is revealed from faith to faith; as it is written, "But the righteous man shall live by faith." (Rom. 1:17)

As we saw in the previous chapter, faith is the action that connects our need to be rescued with God's provision for our rescue. Remember the woman jumping from the burning building into the net below? Although the woman is saved by the net and not merely by the leap from the burning building, she cannot be saved without leaping. Her leap of faith is the action that connects her need with the provision for her rescue.

What Is "Saving Faith"?

Every day we are required to exercise faith in some aspect of our life. My friend John Bisagno, former pastor of First Baptist Church in Houston, observed, "Faith is the very heart of life. You go to a doctor whose name you cannot pronounce. He gives you a prescription you cannot read. You take it to a pharmacist you have never seen. He gives you medicine you do not understand, and yet, you take it!"[13]

Faith is important in this life, but it is essential for the next life. The apostle Paul repeatedly emphasized the importance of personal faith in salvation. The theme of his letter to the Roman Christians is that the *righteousness* of God (a term meaning "a right standing with God") is available to those who have faith in Jesus Christ. Notice how many times Paul uses the word *faith* or *believe* in just six verses of Romans 3:

But now apart from the Law the righteousness of God has been manifested, being witnessed by the Law and the Prophets, even the righteousness of God through *faith* in Jesus Christ for all those who *believe*; for there is no distinction; for all have sinned and fall short of the glory of God, being justified as a gift by His grace through the redemption which is in Christ Jesus; whom God displayed publicly as a propitiation in His blood through *faith* . . . that He would be just and the justifier of the one who has *faith* in Jesus. (vv. 21–26)

Paul was clear that none of us can be saved *by* faith but only *through* faith. What's the difference? Suppose tonight, at seven o'clock, I have a long piece of cable lying on my ottoman in front of my favorite chair. As I munch on my bowl of popcorn, I look at the piece of cable and say, "Where's my favorite television show?" Obviously, that piece of cable can't produce a television show regardless of how long it is. The cable only serves as a connector between the cable box (the transmitter) and my television set (the receiver).

In the same way, faith in and of itself is incapable of producing salvation regardless of how much of it we have. Faith is simply the connector that allows me to receive the forgiveness of my sins that God has "transmitted" through the death of Jesus Christ on the cross. That is why Paul wrote, "For *by grace* you have been saved *through faith*" (Eph. 2:8). We are saved by God's gracious act of sending Christ to be the sacrifice for our sins. But for that gracious act to affect my life, I must receive it through faith.

Here's one final thought about faith that is crucial to understand. Faith is only as reliable as the object of our faith. For example, let's return to my cable analogy. Let's say I have one

> *We are saved by God's gracious act of sending Christ to be the sacrifice for our sins. But for that gracious act to affect my life, I must receive it through faith.*

end of the cable attached to my television set, but the other end is attached to my toaster. It doesn't matter how long or reliable that cable is, I'm not going to be watching any television program that night!

Similarly, neither the amount nor the sincerity of a person's faith determines whether that person will be welcomed by God into heaven. Someone might sincerely attach his or her faith to another religion or to a general feeling that everything will work out in the end. But that object to which he or she has attached his or her faith is no more capable of producing salvation than my toaster is of producing a television picture.

That is why the apostle Paul linked *faith* and *believe* to the gospel of Jesus Christ:

> But to the one who does not work, but *believes* in Him who justifies the ungodly, his *faith* [in Christ] is credited as righteousness. (Rom. 4:5)

A Sober Warning

In this and the previous chapter we have seen that the three major figures of the Christian faith—Jesus Christ, the apostle Peter, and the apostle Paul—believed that faith in Christ alone was God's exclusive way to heaven. Through their words and their ministries they rejected any alternative way for a person to be saved.

While the teachings of the two most prominent apostles (Peter and Paul) and the Son of God Himself (Jesus Christ) should be sufficient to end the discussion on this topic, I want to consider the words of one more contributor to the New Testament: the author of the book of Hebrews.

Although the author's identity is unknown, the situation that led to the writing of this letter is clear. Some Jews who had converted to Christianity were considering returning to Judaism because of mounting pressure from friends and family members. The writer argues unapologetically that Christianity is a superior belief system to Judaism because it has a superior High Priest (Jesus Christ) who offered a superior sacrifice (His own blood) to obtain a superior result (our eternal salvation).

Today, the writer of Hebrews would be labeled as a religious bigot for claiming Christianity is superior to other religions, especially Judaism. Why does he feel it necessary to condemn someone else's sincerely held religious beliefs? Why not allow everyone to find his or her own way to God? Yet the writer of Hebrews warns throughout the letter that abandoning Christianity would result in God's eternal condemnation:

> How much severer punishment do you think he will deserve who has trampled under foot the Son of God, and has regarded as unclean the blood of the covenant by which he was sanctified, and has insulted the Spirit of grace? For we know Him who said, "Vengeance is Mine, I will repay." And again, "The Lord will judge His people." It is a terrifying thing to fall into the hands of the living God. (Heb. 10:29–31)

There are similar stark warnings sprinkled throughout this letter, but the first warning found in Hebrews is the one I want to conclude with:

> For this reason we must pay much closer attention to what we have heard, so that we do not drift away from it. (Heb. 2:1)

I don't know if the writer of Hebrews was a fisherman or just enjoyed sailing on the weekends, but he uses two nautical terms to impress upon us the exclusivity of the gospel of Jesus Christ. The Greek word translated "pay much closer attention" was used to describe tying up a boat to its mooring so that it does not drift away. In other words, the writer is claiming that it is imperative that we "tie up" to the gospel of Jesus Christ or we will drift away from God.

The second phrase that also pictures a sailing vessel is "so that we do not drift away." This term describes a ship that has drifted past a harbor due to the inattention of the sailors. They did not intentionally miss the harbor—they were eager to return home safely. But the sailors allowed themselves to be distracted by other things and missed the narrow opening that would lead them into the secure harbor.

Then, just in case anyone has missed the point, the writer of Hebrews drives it home:

> For if the word spoken through the angels [a reference to the Mosaic law] proved unalterable, and every transgression and disobedience received a just penalty, how will we escape if we neglect so great a salvation? (vv. 2–3)

The writer is saying, "Before you abandon faith in Christ for your salvation and return to Judaism, ask yourself, how do you expect to escape God's promised judgment for everyone who breaks God's laws?" That is a sobering question . . . for all of us.

If you reject—or simply neglect—the one provision God has made for the forgiveness of your sins, then what is your plan for entering into heaven one day? The consistent message of Jesus, the apostles, and all the New Testament writers is clear: there is no other way and there is no other name through which we can be saved other than Jesus Christ.

> *The consistent message of Jesus, the apostles, and all the New Testament writers is clear: there is no other way and there is no other name through which we can be saved other than Jesus Christ.*

7

What about Those Who Have Never Heard?

"It's not *fair!*" my older daughter would protest anytime I administered any punishment for misbehavior, whether it was a spanking in her younger days or the exceedingly more painful confiscation of her car keys when she was a teenager. She was confident that whatever punishment I meted out was excessive for what she viewed as a nonexistent or minor infraction of the house rules.

I realize that some of you have been screaming (at least on the inside) the same charge throughout the pages of this book: "It's not *fair* that God would condemn to an eternity in hell people who have never even heard of Jesus Christ!" That severe punishment seems grossly unjust for people who, for whatever reason, have never been exposed to the good news of Christ's willingness to forgive those who trust in Him for salvation.

Thirty years ago the question was framed this way: "What about the heathen in Africa who have never heard the gospel?" (For some reason, we used to think all the heathen in the world seemed to congregate in Africa.) In other words, what about those in other countries who have not yet heard the gospel?

Today, you do not have to live in a jungle halfway around the world to have missed hearing about Christ. My aforementioned daughter (who is now in her twenties and beyond the years of spankings and key confiscations) told me of an acquaintance from work who had never heard of Adam and Eve or Jesus Christ. It was inconceivable to me that an intelligent young adult living in the Dallas–Fort Worth metroplex—the buckle of the Bible Belt—would be completely unfamiliar with even the names of the First Couple or of Jesus Christ.

As our culture becomes increasingly secular, the question concerning the eternal destiny of those who have never heard the gospel becomes increasingly relevant, especially when we tack on the word *innocent* to the question: "What about the innocent young woman in Syria who has never heard of Jesus Christ? Is she condemned to hell even though she has never had an opportunity to accept or reject the gospel?"

In this chapter I'm going to equip you to know how to answer that question using four biblical propositions that we will explore in detail:

1. Everyone is guilty before God.
2. No one is saved apart from faith in Jesus Christ.
3. Everyone has received a knowledge of God.
4. Anyone who wants further knowledge of Christ will receive it.

Everyone Is Guilty before God

No one can appreciate the Good News without understanding the bad news: we are all guilty before God because of sin. Like a prosecuting attorney, the apostle Paul spends the first three chapters of his letter to the Romans demonstrating the sinfulness of all humanity: the Jews, the gentiles, the religious, and the pagans. In his closing argument Paul declares:

> Are we better than they? Not at all; for we have already charged that both Jews and Greeks are all under sin; as it is written, "There is none righteous, not even one"; . . . For all have sinned and fall short of the glory of God. (Rom. 3:9–10, 23)

The term *righteous* simply means "in a right standing with God." So how many "righteous" people are there on planet Earth? Six times in three verses (Rom. 3:10–12) Paul uses the words "no one" or "not even one." No one is righteous because all of us are guilty. No exceptions.

In your more honest moments you probably don't have any difficulty acknowledging your guilt before God. But what about that young Syrian woman who has never heard about Jesus Christ? What sin has she committed that is so horrible that it warrants spending eternity in hell?

As we saw earlier, every human being has inherited the "sin virus" through Adam:

> Through one man sin entered into the world, and death through sin, and so death spread to all men, because all sinned. (5:12)

The demonstrable fact that everyone eventually dies (including young women in Syria who have never heard the gospel) is proof that everyone has inherited not only the propensity to sin but also the guilt for Adam's sin. If you are tempted to argue that it is not "fair" that we should be condemned for Adam's sin (even though we make the same choice Adam did every day of our lives), then here is something even more "unfair": through the actions of another Man (Jesus Christ), the multitudes who trust in Him are declared righteous.

> For if by the transgression of the one, death reigned through the one, much more those who receive the abundance of grace and of the gift of righteousness will reign in life through the One, Jesus Christ. (v. 17)

Since we explored the reality and origin of our sin in chapter 4, let's focus on the result of our sin: we all deserve the wrath of God.

I admit that it is not popular today to speak of the anger of God or the wrath of God. Few people are insulted by hearing about the love of God, the compassion of God, or even the justice of God. But many people—Christians and non-Christians alike—are offended by any reference to God's wrath. Perhaps in your own conversations with unbelievers, you have even caught yourself focusing on God's love and avoiding any mention of God's "wrath."

In recent years, the Presbyterian Church (USA) dropped the popular hymn "In Christ Alone" from its hymnal because the songwriters Keith Getty and Stuart Townsend refused to replace their lyrics, "On that cross, as Jesus died, the wrath of God was satisfied," to "On that cross, as Jesus died, the love of God was magnified." The committee felt there was something offensive about the idea of Christ dying to satisfy some requirements of an angry God.[1] Thankfully, the songwriters were more interested in theological correctness than political correctness.

136

The Bible clearly refers to the wrath or the anger of God. As the late author Arthur Pink notes, "A study of the concordance will show that there are more references in Scripture to the anger, fury, and wrath of God than there are to his love and tenderness."[2] We should never shy away from communicating this essential aspect of God's character.

In the same conversation in which Jesus told Nicodemus of God's love ("For God so loved the world, that He gave His only begotten Son," John 3:16), Jesus also spoke of the wrath of God:

> He who believes in the Son has eternal life; but he who does not obey the Son will not see life, but *the wrath of God* abides on him. (v. 36)

Similarly, the apostle Paul did not hesitate to write about the reality of God's wrath:

> For *the wrath of God* is revealed from heaven against all ungodliness and unrighteousness of men who suppress the truth in unrighteousness. (Rom. 1:18)

> But if our unrighteousness demonstrates the righteousness of God, what shall we say? *The God who inflicts wrath* is not unrighteous, is He? (3:5)

> Let no one deceive you with empty words, for because of these things *the wrath of God* comes upon the sons of disobedience. (Eph. 5:6)

What do we mean by "the wrath of God"? In the New Testament there are two predominant Greek words that are translated "anger" or "wrath." One of those words is *thumos*, which refers to the explosive kind of rage that we all experience. For example, if someone cuts in front of you on the highway, provokes you with a sarcastic comment, or pushes one of your emotional buttons, you might respond with a volcanic explosion of anger that eventually dissipates.

The other Greek word translated "anger" or "wrath" is *orge*. This is the word Paul uses ten times in the book of Romans to describe God's anger. Leon Morris defines God's anger or wrath, His *orge*, as, "A strong and settled opposition to all that is evil arising out of God's own nature. It is the holy revulsion of God's—being against that which is the contradiction of His holiness."[3] God doesn't suddenly flare up at unbelievers because they have personally offended Him and then quickly get over it and apologize for His outburst!

Instead, God has a consistent opposition and hatred toward all that is evil. Like water building behind a dam, God's anger is continually mounting against all ungodliness. Sometimes that anger spills over onto people's lives when they violate His principles:

> For the wrath of God is revealed from heaven against all ungodliness and unrighteousness of men who suppress the truth in unrighteousness. (Rom. 1:18)

When we violate God's commandments we feel His anger through the natural consequences of disobedience, such as broken relationships, loss of a job, divorce, humiliation, addictions, or illness. While these painful consequences are not always an expression of God's anger, many times they are.

However, the full fury of God's wrath is still building "behind the dam" to be poured out in the future:

Because of your stubbornness and unrepentant heart you are storing up wrath for yourself in the day of wrath and revelation of the righteous judgment of God. (2:5)

The "day of wrath" is that future time in history when God will unleash His judgment against "all ungodliness and unrighteousness of men" (1:18). Paul describes this future event as "the revelation of the righteous judgment of God" (2:5). When does this event occur?

Paul has in mind the same final judgment at the end of time that the apostle John describes in detail in the book of Revelation:

Then I saw a great white throne and Him who sat upon it, from whose presence earth and heaven fled away, and no place was found for them. And I saw the dead, the great and the small, standing before the throne, and books were opened; and another book was opened, which is the book of life; and the dead were judged from the things which were written in the books, according to their deeds.... And if anyone's name was not found written in the book of life, he was thrown into the lake of fire. (Rev. 20:11–12, 15)

The ultimate expression of God's wrath will be His sentencing of every human being who has ever lived into that horrific place of separation from God known as "the lake of fire." The only people who will be exempted from that eternal sentence of death will be those whose names are found in the "book of life"—the record of every individual who has trusted in Jesus Christ as the One who has satisfied the wrath of God.

And that leads to a second truth we can say about all people—including those who have never heard the gospel.

No One Is Saved Apart from Faith in Jesus Christ

A few years ago I was speaking with a Muslim young man who had converted to Christianity and dedicated his life to sharing the gospel with other Muslims. In our conversation he observed, "One of the greatest hindrances in speaking to followers of Islam about Jesus Christ is Christians' unwillingness to use the name 'Allah' instead of 'God' when referring to our heavenly Father. After all, what difference does it really make? Both names refer to the same God."

Many Christians would agree with that man's sentiment. We are repeatedly told that heaven will be populated with a multitude of people who never knew the name of Jesus Christ (much less trusted in Him as Savior) but worshiped a Divine Being whom they called by another name. "Heaven will be much larger than we can imagine," we are told. Even the great Baptist preacher of the nineteenth century, Charles Haddon Spurgeon, embraced the unbiblical idea that the population of heaven will exceed the population of hell:

> Some narrow-minded bigots think that heaven will be a very small place, where there will be a very few people, who went to their chapel or to their church. . . . There will be more in heaven than there are among the lost. God says, that "there will be a number that no man can number who will be saved;" but he never says that there will be a number that no man can number that will be lost. There will be a host beyond all count who will get into heaven.[4]

On what basis do otherwise theologically orthodox Christians who believe that salvation is through faith in Christ alone argue that heaven will include people who do not recognize Jesus as the Son of God but instead know Him by a different name?

Recently, I tried to illustrate to my congregation how ridiculous such an assertion is. "Suppose the church had advertised all week that today's message will be delivered by Dr. David Jeremiah. When you arrived, you looked at the bulletin and saw the title of the message with the name 'Dr. David Jeremiah' beside it. But when the time came for the message I stood up and preached. After the message you approach me and, trying to hide your disappointment, you say, 'Pastor, I thought Dr. Jeremiah was preaching today. Is he ill?' And I reply, 'Not at all. Actually David Jeremiah is just another name I occasionally use to refer to myself. Other times I go by Chuck Swindoll, Joel Osteen, or Jesse Jackson. But we are all the same person!'"

As we saw in the previous chapter, names are important because they represent the essence of a person's being—his character, his deeds, his will, and his personality. While my friend David Jeremiah and I share some similar characteristics—pastors of large churches, graduates of Dallas Theological Seminary, authors of books—we are also two very different people. The name Jesus Christ represents a specific Person who at a point in history surrendered His rights as the Son of God, came to earth in the form of an infant, lived a perfect life, suffered a horrific death on a wooden cross, experienced the full brunt of God's wrath for the sins of the world, and rose from the dead three days after His death.

While Jesus may share similar characteristics with Allah, Krishna, the Buddha, or any number of human prophets or pagan deities, the Lord Jesus Christ is a distinctly different Person. The Bible offers absolutely no hint that salvation is possible through any other means than by faith in this Person who is known by the name Jesus Christ. That is why Peter unapologetically proclaimed:

> And there is salvation in no one else; for there is no other name under heaven that has been given among men by which we must be saved. (Acts 4:12)

The apostle John made the same claim in one of his last letters. This disciple who referred to himself as "the disciple whom Jesus loved" throughout the Gospel he penned wanted his readers to know with certainty whether or not they possessed eternal life:

> These things I have written to you who believe in the name of the Son of God, so that you may know that you have eternal life. (1 John 5:13)

If you wait until you have crossed from this life into eternity to discover whether you will spend eternity in heaven or in hell, then you will have waited one second too long. This is why it is so important for us to share the gospel with a strong sense of urgency and immediacy. No person knows exactly how much time he or she has been given here on this earth. And waiting just one second too long to "believe in the name of the Son of God" could mean the difference between eternal life or eternal death, being separated from God and His love forever.

The Bible offers absolutely no hint that salvation is possible through any other means than by faith in this Person who is known by the name Jesus Christ.

One's salvation should not be a mystery but a reality about which we are absolutely sure. And the only ones who can be certain of their eternal destiny are those who have believed in Jesus Christ.

Everyone Has Received a Knowledge of God

A college professor once constructed an elaborate planetary model of our solar system, depicting the sun and the other planets and their relative distance between one another. A student walked in and, eyeing the model, asked, "Prof, who made this?"

"No one," the professor answered. The student laughed and said, "Come on, Prof. Who constructed this elaborate model?" The professor repeated, "No one."

The student couldn't hide his irritation with his teacher's unresponsiveness. Then the professor added, "If you can go out of this class, look around at nature, and believe this all just happened, then you should have no problem believing that this intricate piece of work could happen without a creator."

Anyone and everyone who has ever lived can know that there is a God without ever reading a Bible or listening to a sermon. This knowledge of God that is readily available to everyone is what we refer to as "natural revelation." The term *natural revelation* identifies the source of the limited information about God that is available to everyone: nature.

In Paul's day, the equivalent of the "heathen in Africa" were called gentiles. These were people who because of their non-Jewishness were unfamiliar with the God of the Scriptures. Some of Paul's audience in Rome wondered if these gentiles were exempt from the wrath of God Paul had described in Romans 1.

How could God condemn people who had never received the commandments of God? How could God sentence to hell people who never had an opportunity to hear the gospel of Jesus Christ?

Without hesitation, Paul declared that these gentiles were just as guilty as the Jews who knew about the God of the Old Testament and had heard the gospel of Jesus Christ. Why?

> For since the creation of the world His invisible attributes, His eternal power and divine nature, have been clearly seen, being understood through what has been made, so that they are without excuse. (Rom. 1:20)

Everyone can look around at the natural world and realize there must be a God who brought it into existence. Furthermore, there are some things nature tells us about this God. For example, creation reveals to us God's "eternal power." I could spend the remainder of the chapter sharing examples of how the universe testifies of God's power, but just consider the vastness of creation.

Astronomers can now view objects 47 billion light years away (one light year is the distance light travels in a year at 186,282 miles per second).[5] If we could travel at the speed of light across our own Milky Way galaxy, it would take us 150,000 years to make the journey. Yet our galaxy is only one of millions we would have to traverse to reach the boundaries of the universe.[6]

How does someone rationally account for the vastness (not to mention the complexity) of the universe? The secularist responds, "It happened by chance." Yet "chance" is not a power but a mathematical probability. For example, if you were to flip a penny in the air, what are the chances it would land heads-up? The mathematical probability is 50-50.

But if indeed the penny landed heads-up, what made it do so? It could have been the force of my thumb, the weight of the penny, the distance the coin traveled, and dozens of other factors. But "chance" would not be one of those factors, because "chance" is not a power but a mathematical prognostication.

Similarly, "chance" has no power to create anything in the universe. Instead, the created world screams out the existence of a Creator. As the psalmist declared,

> The heavens are telling of the glory of God;
> And their expanse is declaring the work of His hands.
> (Ps. 19:1)

Beyond God's "eternal power," Paul asserts that creation also reveals something about God's "divine nature" (Rom. 1:20). While there are some truths about God and His Son, Jesus Christ, that can only be known through the revelation found in the Bible, there are other aspects of God anyone can know about simply by looking at creation. For example, the created world reveals the kindness of God.

When the apostle Paul and Barnabas arrived in Lystra on their first missionary journey, the people started worshiping them as the deities Zeus and Hermes because of the apostles' power to perform miracles. Paul quickly corrected them and pointed them to the true God—a God they had never heard or read about, but One who was clearly evident from creation:

> Men, why are you doing these things? We are also men of the same nature as you, and preach the gospel to you that you should turn from these vain things to a living God, who made the heaven and the earth and the sea and all that is in them. In the generations

gone by He permitted all the nations to go their own ways; and yet He did not leave Himself without witness, in that He did good and gave you rains from heaven and fruitful seasons, satisfying your hearts with food and gladness. (Acts 14:15–17)

The fact that God sends rain regularly to both the just and the unjust, providing people with necessary food regardless of their relationship with Him, reveals the kindness of God.

So often we focus on the things that seem to go wrong in the world—such as famines, earthquakes, floods, and tsunamis. "If God exists, then why does He allow bad things to happen?" the skeptic asks. How do we respond to that question? By pointing out that those events are the exception rather than the rule. Usually rain comes regularly, tectonic plates remain stable, and rivers and oceans stay within their boundaries. So the more perplexing question is, "Why does God allow good things to happen to people in spite of our disobedience or disregard of Him?"

One reason is the kindness of God. If God gave us what we deserved He would strike us dead after our first infraction of His law. But the fact that God not only delays His judgment so that we have an opportunity to receive the gospel but also showers us with gifts such as rain, life, family, friends, and a way to earn a living is evidence of His goodness—evidence that Paul argues should motivate us to turn away from sin and toward God:

Or do you think lightly of the riches of His kindness and tolerance and patience, not knowing that the kindness of God leads you to repentance? (Rom. 2:4)

At the risk of sounding like a sappy greeting card, God sends us a bouquet of beautiful gifts every day to remind us of His

corruptible man and of birds and four-footec
ing creatures. (Rom. 1:22–23)

If you take a course in comparative religi
ties today you will be taught about the "ev
Just as mankind has progressed physicall
through the years, so we have progressed
are told. Secularists claim that man has ev
(the worship of objects) to polytheism (tl
gods) to monotheism (the worship of on
god may be called by a variety of names).

But God's Word reveals a completely diffe
the de-evolution of man's worship. Mank
knowledge of the one true God who reveal
and Eve, but the majority of humanity rejec
and replaced the true God with one of thei
digression of man's spiritual worship may r
worship of a multitude of gods such as tl
hundred million deities in Hinduism, the
or the man-made idols Paul describes in R

However, in our culture, idolatry is muc
bowing before a golden statute one has c
wrote, "Wrong ideas about God are not onl
which the polluted waters of idolatry flow;
idolatrous. The idolater simply imagines thi
acts as if they were true."[8]

When you hear someone say they can't i

has the power to stop evil but doesn't,
sends people to a place of eternal tormer

affection toward us. Yet the majority of mankind ignore those undeserved gifts and begin a downward spiral away from God that Paul describes in Romans 1.

First, the unbeliever *rejects* the knowledge of God received through creation:

> For even though they knew God, they did not honor Him as God or give thanks, but they became futile in their speculations, and their foolish heart was darkened. (v. 21)

Secularists argue that their rejection of God is based on an objective evaluation of scientific evidence that is untainted by religious presuppositions. We may be tempted to believe that they reject the idea of God based on solid evidence from unbiased scientific studies, but actually the opposite is true. Harvard biologist Richard Lewontin conceded in an article for *The New York Review of Books* that he is an evolutionist by default, admitting that his presupposition of materialism and naturalism does not allow for a divine explanation for creation—even if all the evidence points there.

> It is not that the methods and institutions of science somehow compel us to accept a material explanation of the phenomenal world, but, on the contrary, that we are forced by our *a priori* adherence to material causes to create an apparatus of investigation and a set of concepts that produce material explanations, no matter how counter-intuitive, no matter how mystifying to the uninitiated. Moreover, that materialism is absolute, for we cannot allow a Divine Foot in the door.[7]

How's that for objectivity! Lewontin's statement reminds me of a conversation I had last year with David Silverman, president

of American Atheists, before we w
together. "David, is there any evider
that God exists?" I asked.

"Yes," David said. "An end to wo
to rethink my position."

"David, be honest," I pressed. "If
to world hunger, that wouldn't caus
about God."

He grinned and conceded, "No,

We have this fictitious idea that
truth seeker who, if presented with
would turn to God. But Paul says
that keeps an unbeliever from findi
to know God and submit his or her

> *We have this fictitious idea that an unbeliever is a sincere truth seeker who, if presented with enough objective evidence, would turn to God.*

the unbel
the reason
is the sam
find a poli
tant realit
sharing th
reject the
matter ho
message.

In addit
edge of God received through creati
that revelation about the true God
god:

Professing to be wise, they became
glory of the incorruptible God for

and to come to the knowledge of the truth" (1 Tim. 2:3–4). Remember, God's desire is to save as many people as possible, not as few as possible.

While this explanation may answer "What about those who have never heard about Christ?" there is another group of people we wonder about: those who could never believe in Jesus Christ. For example, are those who lived before Jesus died out of luck? If faith in Jesus Christ is the only way to be saved, then how were people saved prior to the death and resurrection of Christ?

And what about those people who have no capacity to believe regardless of when they were born? Are infants or mentally impaired individuals condemned to an eternity in hell because they could never comprehend—much less believe in—the message of Christ? If you reflexively answer no to such a question, then on what basis do you believe God will accept these people into heaven? If God can allow into heaven people who have never trusted in Christ, doesn't that represent a crack in the doctrine of exclusivity? Shouldn't God also be willing and capable of allowing others into heaven as well?

How Were People before Christ Saved?

Let's first tackle the question of those who lived before the time of Christ. When we think of those who lived in Old Testament times, we naturally think of well-known names like Adam, Eve, Noah, Sarah, Moses, Esther, and David. But we need to expand that list to include the multitudes of people—unknown to us—who lived between the time of Adam and Noah, to all those who drowned in the flood, to the average Israelite who lived in bondage in Egypt, to the Amorites and Hittites, and all the other billions of people who populated the planet before Christ ever died on a wooden cross outside of Jerusalem.

It is one thing to argue that God will send unbelievers today the information about Christ they need to be saved, regardless of where they live. But how could unbelievers who lived prior to AD 33 logically be saved by a Christ who had not yet offered Himself as a sacrifice for our sins? And if you argue that this group of people had the ability to be saved apart from Jesus Christ, then why doesn't God allow an alternate path to Himself today if He truly desires to save as many people as possible?

A Case Study: Abraham

The apostle Paul answers those legitimate questions in Romans 4 by examining in depth exactly how Abraham, a man who lived two thousand years before the coming of Christ, obtained salvation. The theme of Paul's letter to the Christians in Rome is found in the opening chapter:

> I am not ashamed of the gospel, for it is the power of God for salvation to everyone who believes, to the Jew first and also to the Greek. (Rom. 1:16)

The fear of being labeled "intolerant" or "narrow-minded" did not prevent Paul from boldly declaring the good news about Jesus Christ to everyone, because the apostle was convinced that only through Christ could anyone escape God's judgment. Paul, a Jew himself, insisted that the message of Christ was the only hope of salvation for the Jews, as well as for the gentiles.

Of course, this message enraged Paul's fellow Jews, who were convinced that their commitment to the Jewish laws and rituals was sufficient to place them in a right relationship with God. Anticipating their opposition to his message, Paul beats them to the punch by using Abraham as the supreme example that salvation has always been received by faith rather than achieved through works.

Why Abraham? He was the father of their nation. But beyond being the progenitor of the Israelites, Abraham was revered by the Jewish people as the supreme example of righteousness . . . and for good reason. Think of all the ways Abraham exhibited his faith in God:

- In Genesis 12, God commanded Abraham to leave everything familiar to him, pack up his family, and head to a foreign land. Without argument, Abraham picked up his tent and went.
- In Genesis 13, Abraham willingly allowed himself to get "taken" in a real estate transaction with his nephew Lot in order to preserve peace in the family.
- In Genesis 17, Abraham was the first Jew ever to be circumcised as a sign of his relationship with God.
- In Genesis 18, when God announced His plan to destroy the wicked cities of Sodom and Gomorrah, Abraham pleaded with God to spare the lives of any righteous people in those cities.
- In Genesis 22, Abraham submitted to God's command to offer his son Isaac as a human sacrifice. Although God ultimately provided a substitute sacrifice at the last moment, Abraham's willingness to obey God would be heralded for thousands of years to come as the supreme example of righteousness.

No wonder the Jews pointed to Abraham as an example of someone who achieved righteousness (a right standing with God) through his good works. "But wait a minute," Paul warns. "What does the Old Testament have to say about Abraham's righteousness? Was it obtained by good works or by faith?"

> If Abraham was justified by works, he has something to boast about, but not before God. For what does the Scripture say? "Abraham believed God, and it was credited to him as righteousness." (Rom. 4:2–3)

Paul is referring to the signal spiritual event in Abraham's life: when God declared him to be righteous. Abraham had just completed a successful battle against the kings of the East in order to free his nephew, Lot, who had been taken hostage. Fearful of some kind of retaliation by those powerful monarchs, Abraham became depressed. "What if I'm attacked and lose all of my wealth? Worse, what if I lose my life?" the old patriarch worried.

So the Lord encouraged His servant with these words:

> Do not fear, Abram,
> I am a shield to you;
> Your reward shall be very great. (Gen. 15:1)

Abraham understood that the reward that God was referring to was the promise of being the father of a great nation, as evidenced by his response to God's promise:

> O Lord GOD, what will You give me, since I am childless? (v. 2)

So God took Abraham out one evening to do some stargazing. "Count the stars," the Lord commanded. "So shall your descendants be" (v. 5). In other words, God was saying to him, "See if you can calculate how many millions of stars there are in the sky. That's how many descendants you will have."

How did Abraham respond to that promise? He responded in a way that would change the trajectory of his earthly life and eternal destiny:

> Then he believed in the LORD; and He reckoned it to him as righteousness. (v. 6)

Fast-forward two thousand years to the time Paul is writing his letter to the Roman Christians explaining how Abraham was justified (a word meaning "to declare to be righteous"). Paul argues that Abraham's salvation was not obtained through his good works, as the Jews believed, but through his faith. And to prove his point to his Jewish audience, Paul reaches back to Genesis 15:

> For what does the Scripture say? "Abraham believed God, and it was credited to him as righteousness." (Rom. 4:3)

In this simple verse we discover how those, like Abraham, who lived before Christ were saved. It's the very same way people living after Christ are saved.

Abraham's Salvation Was Received through Faith

"Abraham believed God" (Rom. 4:3). Abraham believed in more than the existence of God; he believed in the promise of God. The context of Genesis 15 clearly identifies the promise to be that Abraham would be the father of a great nation.

But the promise included more than that. Since the time of Adam and Eve's sin, mankind had been looking for a Deliverer who would break sin's stranglehold on the world. Eve mistakenly thought her newborn son Cain was that Deliverer (Gen. 4:1). It is the same Deliverer Jacob spoke of to his sons while on his deathbed in Egypt (49:10–12). It is the same Deliverer John the Baptist announced when he exclaimed, "Behold, the Lamb of God who takes away the sin of the world" (John 1:29). That Deliverer is the Lord Jesus Christ.

I'm not suggesting that Abraham's faith included a perfect understanding of Jesus Christ, but Abraham's faith included the anticipation of something more than a multitude of descendants. He believed that among those descendants would be the One who would provide a means by which people could be reconciled to God.

How do I know that? While making the same argument that salvation is through faith and not works to another group of people, the apostle Paul again used the example of Abraham's faith, but he also gave more insight into its content:

> Even so Abraham believed God, and it was reckoned to him as righteousness. Therefore, be sure that it is those who are of faith who are sons of Abraham. The Scripture, foreseeing that God would justify the Gentiles by faith, preached the gospel beforehand to Abraham, saying, "All the nations will be blessed in you." So then those who are of faith are blessed with Abraham, the believer. (Gal. 3:6–9)

Paul says that Abraham heard and believed in the good news God preached to him: people would be made right with God through faith, not through their works.

We don't know how much actual knowledge Abraham, Moses, David, or other major figures in the Old Testament had about Jesus Christ. They certainly had more information than the average Jew who lived in bondage in Egypt for four hundred years or wandered in the wilderness for forty years. And those Israelites possessed more information than the humans who roamed the earth in the years between Noah and Moses. But a full understanding of Christ was not necessary for those living before Christ to exercise saving faith. Why?

> *Paul says that Abraham heard and believed in the good news God preached to him: people would be made right with God through faith, not through their works.*

Because people living before and after Christ are never saved *by* their faith, but *through* their faith, as we saw in chapter 4. Faith is the conduit through which God's forgiveness is received into our lives. Remember the illustration of leaping from a burning building into a net? It is the net, not the leap into the net, that saves a person. Yet without jumping, the person would not be rescued.

So if Abraham's faith did not save him, how was he saved?

Abraham's Salvation Was Based on the Death of Jesus Christ

Many people assume that people who lived before Christ must have been saved in a different way than those of us who live after Christ: through obedience to God's commands, through religious rituals like circumcision, or through the offering of animal sacrifices. But Paul went to great lengths to demonstrate that Abraham's works and rituals were not sufficient to make him right with God. Even the animal sacrifices commanded later under the Mosaic law were powerless to remove the permanent stain of people's sins.

It is impossible for the blood of bulls and goats to take away sins. (Heb. 10:4)

The animal sacrifices of the Old Testament simply served as constant reminders to the Israelites of their need for a permanent, once-for-all solution to their sin problem. The sacrificial death of Jesus Christ, the Lamb of God, was God's ultimate solution for man's greatest problem.

When Christ appeared as a high priest of the good things to come, He entered through the greater and more perfect tabernacle, not made with hands, that is to say, not of this creation; and not through the blood of goats and calves, but through His own blood, He entered the holy place once for all, having obtained eternal redemption. (9:11–12)

"Eternal redemption." Think about what that means:

- No more sacrifices to be offered year after year to cover over the stain of sin that keeps reappearing.
- No more trying to earn God's favor by keeping an impossible list of rules.
- No more fear of facing the eternal wrath of an angry God.

Jesus ended all of this through His death for our sins.

"That's great for those who lived after Christ died, but how were the sins of people forgiven before Christ's death?" you ask. Answer: their sins were forgiven the very same way yours and mine are—through the death of Jesus Christ. Regardless of when people lived, the blood of Jesus Christ is the only "spiritual detergent" that can remove the stain of sin.

During the time period before Christ died, I like to say that people were saved "on credit." Let me explain what I mean. Suppose you go to Target and select a new, flat-screen television set that costs $995. At the checkout counter you whip out your MasterCard and give it to the cashier. She swipes the card, returns it to you, and you walk out of the store with your new set.

How is it that you can hand that cashier a worthless piece of plastic and receive something worth nearly a thousand dollars? While your plastic credit card has no value in itself, it does represent a promise to pay in the future. Thirty days later, when the bill comes due, you are required to make the payment.

From the time of Adam and Eve's sin in the garden until the death of Christ, people handed to God various "spiritual credit cards" that demonstrated their faith that God would forgive their sins. None of these acts—obedience to God's commands, rituals, or sacrifices—were sufficient to cleanse people from sins, but they were sufficient for them to immediately obtain God's forgiveness until Christ's death would provide the payment for our sin debt. It is not coincidental that one of Jesus's final cries from the cross was "It is finished!" (John 19:30), which comes from a single Greek word meaning "paid in full."

When Abraham looked at the innumerable stars and believed the promise God had given, the Bible says that Abraham's faith was "reckoned . . . to him as righteousness" (Gen. 15:6). The word *reckoned* is an accounting term that means "credited." When Abraham, like any other person who lived before Christ, demonstrated faith in the revelation God gave him, God exchanged that faith for righteousness—a right standing with God—until the bill for that righteousness was paid by Jesus Christ.

Since the time of Christ's death, people have been declared righteous by God when they demonstrate faith in Christ's death for their sins. And as we have seen, no one since the time of Christ can be saved without trusting in the death of Jesus Christ for the forgiveness of his or her sins.

But regardless of when people live, we are all made right with God in the same way. The means of salvation is faith, and the basis of our salvation is the death of Jesus Christ.

So, What about Children?

One of the most painful parts of any pastor's ministry is trying to offer consolation to parents who have lost a young child through illness or accident. If the parents are Christians, they naturally want to know, "Will I see my child again in heaven?"

Perhaps you have wondered the same thing because you have experienced the loss of a child or grandchild, or you know someone who has. The question can be expanded to include adults who were mentally challenged and were therefore "childlike" when they died. Will they be in heaven?

Of course, anyone with an ounce of compassion would want to reassure parents who have endured that kind of heartache that without question their child is with God. What can we say to encourage them? Beyond our desire to offer comfort, is there any biblical reason to think that infants and young children who died before they were old enough to exercise faith in Christ are saved? If so, then why does God grant them salvation apart from faith in Christ and not do the same for others?

This issue is complicated by the fact that there is no definitive passage in the Bible that clearly states what happens to infants and children when they die. If we could cite a verse that said after their death children automatically go into the presence of Jesus, then we could rest in that assurance. Likewise, if the Bible claimed that children who never called upon Christ for salvation were eternally damned, we would wrestle with that claim but have to accept it.

Although there is no single passage that clearly spells out the eternal destiny of children (and by extension, those who are mentally impaired and are therefore "childlike") who die before trusting in Christ, I believe there are five biblical truths that—when taken together—strongly argue that they are welcomed into heaven.

God Has a Special Love for Children

God's love and concern for every child begins before that child is born. From the moment of conception (and in the foreknowledge of God, even before that), God views that child as a human being, even while he or she is being formed in the mother's womb.

David expressed God's design and care for his life long before he was actually born:

> For You formed my inward parts;
> You wove me in my mother's womb.
> I will give thanks to You, for I am fearfully and wonderfully made;
> Wonderful are Your works,
> And my soul knows it very well.

My frame was not hidden from You,
When I was made in secret,
And skillfully wrought in the depths of the earth;
Your eyes have seen my unformed substance;
And in Your book were all written
The days that were ordained for me,
When as yet there was not one of them.
    (Ps. 139:13–16)

David's words reveal that a fertilized egg inside a mother's womb is more than a biological blob but is rather a human life uniquely designed by God ("skillfully wrought") whose destiny has been planned by Him ("the days that were ordained for me").

Because God is intimately involved in every detail of a child's life, it should be no surprise that He values the lives of children and grieves over their deaths. Listen to God's condemnation of Judah for offering her children as burnt sacrifices to the pagan god Molech:

Moreover, you took your sons and daughters whom you had borne to Me and sacrificed them to idols to be devoured. Were your harlotries so small a matter? You slaughtered My children and offered them up to idols by causing them to pass through the fire. (Ezek. 16:20–21)

God cites this cruelty toward children (whom He calls "My children") as a primary reason He allowed the pagan Babylonians to overtake His own nation and hold them captive for seventy years.

Jesus, the Son of God, reflected through both His words and His actions the special place children hold in God's heart. On one occasion, Jesus's disciples asked the Lord who would be greatest in the kingdom of God:

> And He called a child to Himself and set him before them, and said, "Truly I say to you, unless you are converted and become like children, you will not enter the kingdom of heaven. Whoever then humbles himself as this child, he is the greatest in the kingdom of heaven." (Matt. 18:2–4)

While it is true that Jesus was using this specific child to demonstrate a spiritual truth, it is also true that this analogy doesn't work if the child Jesus selected was destined for hell if he died as a child. There is nothing in this story that suggests Jesus chose this child over another child for any particular reason. Through His action, Jesus was indicating that all children are going to be in heaven.

On another occasion, some parents brought their children to Jesus so that He might bless their children. "Jesus doesn't have time for this kind of foolishness," the disciples barked.

But when Jesus saw this He was indignant and said to them:

> "Permit the children to come to Me; do not hinder them; for the kingdom of God belongs to such as these. Truly I say to you, whoever does not receive the kingdom of God like a child will not enter it at all." And He took them in His arms and began blessing them, laying His hands on them. (Mark 10:14–16)

Once again Jesus was using children as an illustration of the humility necessary to receive God's gift of salvation. But the illustration is nonsensical if God does not welcome children into heaven if they die while too young to comprehend the gospel.

Additionally, Jesus's blessing of these children tells us a great deal about how God views the spiritual condition and destiny of children. As pastor John MacArthur observes:

> I don't know of any place in the New Testament in which Jesus blesses "nonbelievers." There's no place in which Jesus blesses the "cursed" or the "damned." . . . Jesus blessed those in His arms because from heaven's perspective, they were counted among the blessed righteous ones whose rightful eternal home was heaven.[1]

God Views the Inherited Sin of Children Differently Than the Willful Sin of Adults

Because of Adam's original rebellion against God, every person since that time has been infected with the sin virus. The apostle Paul explained both the transmission and the consequences of that virus in Romans 5:12:

> Through one man sin entered into the world, and death through sin, and so death spread to all men, because all sinned.

Physical death is the proof that we have contracted the sin virus, and the fact that everyone dies—including children—is proof that no one is immune to this disease.

Nevertheless, God distinguishes between children's inherited sin (over which they had no choice) and the willful disobedience of adults. God does not hold children accountable for the sins of their parents or the first parents, Adam and Eve. God declared that people are guilty for their own sins, not for the sins of others:

> The person who sins will die. The son will not bear the punishment for the father's iniquity, nor will the father bear the punishment for the son's iniquity; the righteousness of the

righteous will be upon himself, and the wickedness of the wicked will be upon himself. (Ezek. 18:20)

Parents often ask me about the age of accountability for children, meaning, "At what age are children responsible for their own sins?" While the term *age of accountability* is not found in the Bible, the principle is. As long as a child is not able to distinguish between good and evil, he or she is not responsible for the corruption inherited from Adam or the sins he or she personally commits.

We see that truth illustrated in the story of God's judgment against Israel for her unbelief. Although God had promised to give the land of Canaan to His chosen people, they chose to believe the negative report of ten of the twelve spies whom they sent into the land to determine whether they could overtake the Canaanites who inhabited it (Num. 13).

God was so infuriated with their unbelief that He swore that, with the exception of the two spies who gave a positive report (Joshua and Caleb), "Not one of these men, this evil generation, shall see the good land which I swore to give your fathers" (Deut. 1:35). The unbelieving Israelites would die in the wilderness instead of inheriting the land God had promised them.

But God exempted one group of Israelites from His punishment:

Moreover, your little ones who you said would become a prey, and your sons, who this day have no knowledge of good or evil, shall enter there, and I will give it to them and they shall possess it. (v. 39)

Although these children were infected with sin because of Adam's original rebellion, God did not condemn them because they had "no knowledge of good or evil."

Children Have Not Rejected God's Revelation

Because the Israelite children had no ability to distinguish between good and evil, they had no ability to be charged with the same offense as their parents: unbelief. In the Bible the sin of unbelief is not simply failing to believe God; it is the deliberate choice *not* to believe what God has said. Unbelief is the willful rejection of God's revelation.

> *Unbelief is the willful rejection of God's revelation.*

The writer of Hebrews uses the Israelites' experience in the wilderness as an illustration of the seriousness of unbelief:

> And to whom did He swear that they would not enter His rest, but to those who were disobedient? So we see that they were not able to enter because of *unbelief.* (Heb. 3:18–19)

Note that the sin of "unbelief" prevented them from entering "His rest." The Bible is clear: the consequence of a person's unbelief—the deliberate choice not to believe what God has said—is that he or she is not able to enter into heaven. The writer of Hebrews makes this application to all of us:

> Take care, brethren, that there not be in any one of you an evil, *unbelieving* heart that falls away from the living God. (v. 12)

The adult Israelites had done more than simply fail to believe God's promises (something their children failed to do as well because of their intellectual limitations). These adults had decidedly rejected God's promise. The writer of Hebrews, quoting Psalm 95, describes this willful rejection of God's truth as a hardening of one's heart:

171

Today, if you hear His voice,
Do not harden your hearts as when they provoked Me,
As in the day of trial in the wilderness
Where your fathers tried Me by testing Me,
And saw My works for forty years. (vv. 7–9)

The Israelites had seen God's power displayed continuously through the ten plagues He sent against Egypt, the miraculous parting of the Red Sea, and His supernatural provision of food and water for them in the wilderness. Yet they willfully rejected these revelations of God's power and chose not to believe God's promise.

Similarly, Paul says that unbelievers are "without excuse" because of their conscious choice to reject God's truth:

> For the wrath of God is revealed from heaven against all ungodliness and unrighteousness of men who suppress the truth in unrighteousness. . . . For since the creation of the world His invisible attributes, His eternal power and divine nature, have been clearly seen, being understood through what has been made, so that they are without excuse. (Rom. 1:18, 20)

As we saw in chapter 7, no one will ever go to hell for not believing in a Christ of whom they have never heard. Instead, those who never hear the gospel of Jesus Christ will be judged by God for rejecting the revelation about God they *have* received.

Let me illustrate the difference between failing to believe the truth and willfully rejecting the truth. Imagine a driver who is caught in a flash flood driving home from work. He never turned on his radio to hear the warning about the coming storm and perishes in the flood. Contrast him to the driver who hears the weather reports and the pleas from officials to stay off the road

172

but decides to ignore those warnings and also dies in the flood. While it's true that both drivers failed to heed the weather warnings, we sympathize with the first driver because he never heard the warning. However, the second driver made the willful choice to reject the information he received.

Because infants and children do not possess the ability to "hear" God's warnings and comprehend His offer of salvation, God does not condemn them as He does those who willfully harden their hearts against His truth.

Salvation Is Based on God's Grace, Not Our Faith

"I want to believe that children who die are in heaven, but how does that work if they have never trusted in Christ as their Savior?" Frankly, this is a question I have struggled with. If faith in Christ is the basis by which everyone else in the world must be saved, then how is God able to bend the rules for children? For many years, the best answer I could come up with was, "God is a merciful God who will do the right thing."

However, one day I suddenly realized there is a very simple answer to the question, "How are children who have never trusted in Christ saved?" They are saved the same way those who lived before Christ were saved. And it's the same way people are saved today: by God's grace.

> For by grace you have been saved through faith; and that not of yourselves, it is the gift of God; not as a result of works, so that no one may boast. (Eph. 2:8–9)

The fact that a child is not able to exercise faith is really no problem because no one is saved "by faith." Instead we are saved "by grace . . . through faith." As we have seen in previous chapters, God's gracious act of sending Christ to die for our sins is the basis for our salvation, and faith is simply the means by which we access that salvation.

You may wonder why God doesn't extend this grace to everyone automatically, without the need for personal faith. The answer is that God distinguishes between adults who have willfully rejected His revelation and children who have never willfully rejected God's truth.

Let's return to our illustration of the woman standing on the window ledge of the burning building who decides to exercise faith by jumping into the net the firefighters have provided. The woman is saved by the net, not by her jump. Her jump would have been meaningless and even fatal if no net were waiting for her below. She was saved from the flames not by her act of jumping but by the net that caught her.

Now let's change the story a little. Suppose a firefighter is searching the apartment of a burning building and finds a three-year-old child. Soon, the entire apartment erupts into flames and there is no way out. The firefighter gathers the child into his arms, walks out onto the ledge, and holds the toddler in his arms as he leaps into the waiting net below.

Both the adult in the first example who jumped by herself and the child in the second example were both saved by the net provided by the firefighters. Just because the child was incapable of jumping into the net herself does not change the fact that she was saved the same way the adult was saved: by the net.

Similarly, the only way anyone can escape the fire of God's deserved judgment is through the "safety net" God has provided: the sacrificial death of His Son. Children who are incapable of exercising faith (in contrast to adults who are unwilling to exercise faith) are carried in the arms of God into heaven.

The Promise of 2 Samuel 12:21–23

Most people are familiar with the sordid story of King David's tryst with Bathsheba, the wife of Uriah, one of David's soldiers. Their one-night stand led to an unwanted pregnancy and a kingdom scandal that included David's decision to arrange for Uriah's murder as part of the cover-up.

Eventually, David's twin sins of adultery and murder were exposed, and David repented and received God's forgiveness. However, that forgiveness did not exempt David from the painful consequences of his disobedience, which included a divided kingdom, a disloyal son, and eventually a dead child.

The child, who was the product of David and Bathsheba's affair, became ill immediately after birth. David pleaded with God to heal his son, refusing to eat anything while his son lay dying.

But once David received word that his infant son had died, his demeanor and actions changed dramatically. He bathed, put on fresh clothes, and began to eat again. His servants, perplexed by this sudden change, asked the king, in so many words, "Why did you fast and weep while your child was alive but now you are going on with your life when your child has died?" (2 Sam. 12:21).

David replied, "While the child was still alive, I fasted and wept; for I said, 'Who knows, the LORD may be gracious to me, that the child may live.' But now he has died; why should I fast? Can I bring him back again? *I will go to him, but he will not return to me*" (vv. 22–23).

David knew that as long as his son was alive there was a reason to mourn and plead with God for his son's healing. But now that God had chosen to take his son, no amount of prayer and fasting would bring the son back. The knowledge that David would one day "go to" his son gave him the motivation to quit mourning and get on with his life.

So, where did David's infant son go when he died? If the child was sent to hell—and David would eventually "go to him" in hell—then that would be reason for David to mourn even more! If (as some have suggested) David was simply acknowledging he would die like his son died, then that would not be a motivation for celebration either. The only logical explanation is that David believed his infant son had been ushered into the presence of God and eventually David would join him there.

I'll admit that by itself this incident from David's life doesn't prove anything definitively about the destination of children who die. But when you add David's words to the other truths we have seen in this chapter, I believe we can say with confidence that children (and others who are mentally incapable of comprehending the gospel) who die are graciously welcomed by God into His heaven.

9

Simple Answers to Complex Questions

We have looked in depth at biblical support for the doctrine of the exclusivity of Jesus Christ for salvation throughout the Old Testament, the teachings of Jesus, and the writings of the New Testament apostles. We have also explored some of the natural questions that arise in people's minds (perhaps including your own) about this issue.

My purpose in the previous chapters was to explain that the doctrine of the exclusivity of Christ is essential to the Christian message. Hopefully, our in-depth look at this issue has convinced you—or reinforced to you—the veracity of the claim that faith in Christ for salvation is not just a way to escape God's judgment but is the *only* way to escape God's judgment.

But in this final chapter I want to change audiences. I'm imagining a situation in which you are having a discussion with someone who is questioning the exclusivity of Christianity. That "someone" might be . . .

> a stranger you are seated next to on a plane,
>
> a friend or family member with whom you have been sharing your faith, or
>
> your child in college who is troubled by the implications of an exclusive gospel.

I have learned that one way to communicate effectively on television—especially in a debate—is to talk in sound bites. If you launch into a long diatribe that lasts more than sixty seconds, the host will cut you off. Why? Producers realize that viewers have very short attention spans.

So do the people we converse with about the most important topic of all. That is why I have devoted this last chapter to distilling the information we have covered into brief responses you can use when confronted with the seven most common questions and objections to the claim that trusting in Christ as one's Savior is the only way a person will be welcomed into heaven.

"You Are Being Intolerant"

A generation or two ago, *tolerance* meant showing respect for people with whom you disagree. Inherent in that definition is a willingness to disagree with another person's point of view. For example, if you are a right-wing Republican you would not say, "I tolerate the beliefs of Rush Limbaugh." For the most part, you would wholeheartedly endorse his perspective.

However, you would probably have a completely different attitude toward the beliefs of Hillary Clinton. Although you would probably disagree with her on most issues, hopefully you would respect her right to voice her opinions and, if you were ever in her presence, would treat her in a civil manner. That's tolerance.

There is no particular virtue in acting respectfully toward a person who voices a viewpoint with which you agree or have no opinion on yourself. Tolerance assumes that you have judged the other person's viewpoint to be wrong but have chosen to respect that person's right to be wrong.

However, today many understand the word *tolerance* to mean the acceptance of all ideas and opinions as equally valid. To be "tolerant" means to refuse to label any viewpoint as "right" or "wrong"—especially when it comes to moral behavior or religious beliefs. Of course, believing that all viewpoints are equally valid can lead to some illogical conclusions.

> *Tolerance assumes that you have judged the other person's viewpoint to be wrong but have chosen to respect that person's right to be wrong.*

As I point out in my book *Outrageous Truth*, we have to differentiate between objective truth and relative truth.[1] For example, suppose a teacher returns an exam to her students and one of the students notices that she has marked incorrect his answer to the question, "What is the temperature at which water freezes?" "Why did you say my answer is incorrect?" the student asks. "Because you answered thirty-seven degrees and the correct answer is thirty-two degrees," the teacher replies.

The student protests, "Well, that is your opinion." He turns to his other classmates and asks, "How many of you agree with me that the correct answer is thirty-seven degrees?" Half of the students raise their hands. The student then says to the teacher, "Why do you think your opinion is more valid than ours? You are being intolerant!"

Is the student correct? Is his opinion about the freezing temperature of water just as valid as the teacher's? Is the teacher demonstrating intolerance by marking his answer as wrong? Of course not! The freezing temperature of water is not debatable. The correct answer is based on objective truth.

Now, suppose a student says to the teacher, "Please turn up the air conditioner because it's too hot in here." The teacher responds, "We will leave it where it is because the temperature is just right." Is the student or the teacher correct about the "right" temperature? Obviously, there is no right or wrong answer to the question of what is the most comfortable room temperature. The answer falls under the heading of "relative truth" based on opinion, not objective truth.

At the core of most religions is an attempt to answer the question, "How can a person have a right relationship with God?" Unfortunately, a growing number of people believe that the answer to that question falls under the heading of opinion (like comfortable room temperature) rather than objective truth (like the freezing temperature of water). The result is that Christians who maintain that faith in Christ is the only way to heaven are labeled as "intolerant" for insisting that their opinion is objective truth rather than relative opinion. Yet holding such a position is no more intolerant than insisting that thirty-two degrees is the freezing point of water.

"Exclusivity Encourages Hatred toward People of Other Faiths"

You've no doubt heard the claim that "most of the atrocities in human history were caused by people who believed that their religion was the only true religion." How are we to respond to such a charge? Let me suggest three facts you need to point out to people who level this accusation.

First, it is true that horrible things have been done—and continue to be done—in the name of religion. For example, when followers of radical Islam behead "unbelievers" (those who refuse to worship Allah), they are following the example of their spiritual leader, Muhammad, who beheaded six hundred Jewish males who would not support him in battle. Muslims can point to many "sword verses" in the Quran that command followers of Islam to kill the "infidels."[2]

In contrast to Muhammad, the founder of the Christian faith—Jesus Christ—was known as the "Prince of Peace" who never killed anyone. Instead of warring against His enemies who ultimately crucified Him, Jesus prayed, "Father, forgive them; for they do not know what they are doing" (Luke 23:34). Unlike the Quran, the New Testament does not contain a single verse in which Christians are called upon to commit violence against non-Christians. The message of the Quran is "Kill unbelievers," while the message of the New Testament is "Convert unbelievers." Big difference. Some might object to this characterization of the Quran by pointing out verses in which Muhammad encourages peace and love toward non-Muslims. However, Muslim scholars use "the law of abrogation" to interpret the Quran. This principle says that the later verses in the Quran replace the earlier verses. The "peace verses" that correspond to Muhammad's earlier life have been replaced by the "war verses" that correspond to the prophet's later life.

Second, we should acknowledge that there are some dark chapters in Christian history in which atrocities were committed in the name of Christianity. Yet those atrocities need to be placed in some perspective. For example, some people cite the Inquisition as an example of the hatred that exclusivity promotes. Historian Henry Kamen, a leading authority on the Spanish Inquisition, estimates that "a maximum of three thousand persons may have suffered death during the entire history of the tribunal."[3] To put that figure in perspective, as many people were killed by Islamic terrorists on the single day of September 11, 2001, than during the entire 350 years of the Inquisition.

The Crusades are also used as an example of Christian violence. Yet history reveals that the Crusades were a response (admittedly a wrong response) to four hundred years of Muslim aggression that preceded them. Most importantly, the followers of Muhammad were acting in accordance to their founder's command to kill unbelievers. The Crusaders were acting in opposition to the teaching of their founder, Jesus Christ.

Finally, it should be pointed out that insisting that Christ is the only way to heaven—if true—is a demonstration of love, not hatred, toward unbelievers. Here is an example you could share with someone who honestly believes it is hateful to suggest that faith in Christ is the only way to escape God's judgment.

Suppose I walk by your house and see that it is on fire. I bang on your front door and there is no response, so I kick in the door and find that you are groping through the smoke trying to find a way out. I say, "Follow me. Every other exit is blocked, and there is only one way out." Would you accuse me of being hateful for trying to lead you to safety? Would you charge me with being intolerant because I insisted there is only one way out of the house?

The only reason I would try to rescue you is because I care about you. And the only reason I would insist there is only one way out of the house would be that, in fact, there is only one way out of the house.

No person with whom I have shared that illustration has ever had an argument with which to counter. Why? Most unbelievers— and many Christians—think the answer to the question, "How can I be saved from God's judgment?" is a matter of personal opinion rather than objective truth. Since the Bible teaches the answer to that question is just as absolute as the freezing temperature of water, then the most loving thing I can do for another person is share the correct answer with him or her.

"All Religions Teach Essentially the Same Thing"

Here are two responses you can give to the trite—and untrue— claim that, at their core, all religions have the same message.

First, the only people who make such a claim are those who are ignorant of the teachings of the major world religions. For example, those religions that claim Abraham as their spiritual ancestor—Judaism, Christianity, and Islam—are resolute in their teaching of monotheism (the existence of one God). By contrast, Hinduism posits there are millions of gods. Buddhism denies the existence of a personal God and instead sees whatever god there is as the sum total of all creation.

183

Various religions also offer differing theories about the life after death. Hinduism teaches that we are trapped in an endless cycle of life, death, and rebirth. Mormonism teaches differing levels of heaven for almost all of humanity except the worst of the worst of humankind, who are dispatched to hell. However, in Mormonism, even the inhabitants of hell have the opportunity to repent while in hell and inherit one of the levels of heaven. Christianity teaches that after death there is no more opportunity for repentance and that every person's eternal destiny is fixed.

Additionally, the world religions differ on humanity's basic dilemma. Hinduism identifies humanity's chief flaw as a failure to recognize our own deity, resulting in an endless cycle of birth, death, and rebirth. Buddha, a dissatisfied follower of Hinduism, believed humanity's problem was selfishness that could only be eradicated by following the Noble Eightfold Path.

Islam teaches that humanity's problem is our failure to keep the laws of Allah as revealed in the Quran. Judaism teaches that humanity's sinfulness is reflected by our failure to obey the laws of a different God—Yahweh—that are revealed in the Old Testament.

By contrast, Christianity teaches that humanity's problem is much more severe. All people have inherited a defective "internal operating system" that alienates them from God. Furthermore, no efforts to eradicate or rehabilitate humanity's rebellious nature that is opposed to God will succeed. As the apostle Paul wrote, "All have sinned and fall short of the glory of God" (Rom. 3:23).

And that reality leads to a second response to the claim that "all religions teach basically the same thing." A religion doesn't have to be all wrong to be wrong. You can look at almost any of the major world religions and find some kernel of truth in them about God or mankind. That should not surprise us. A counterfeit bill can resemble a legitimate piece of currency, but it is still counterfeit if it was not created by the US Treasury and fails to meet 100 percent of the exacting qualifications for an authentic bill. In fact, the more closely it resembles an authentic bill, the more likely it is to be accepted by unsuspecting victims.

The Bible teaches that other religions are manufactured by Satan in order to deceive people and lead them away from the truth (Ps. 106:36–37; Gal. 1:6–9). But although other religions may resemble Christianity in some ways, there is one vast difference between the teachings of every other world religion and Christianity.

At the core of every religion in the world is an attempt to answer the question, "How can a person have a right relationship with God?" All other religions answer that question with some program of self-rehabilitation that requires keeping a set of rules or engaging in an endless cycle of religious rituals.

> *The fact that Christianity offers an exclusive, unique answer to humanity's greatest dilemma is one of the strongest arguments for the veracity of the Christian message.*

By contrast, Christianity is the only religion that answers the question, "By God's grace." Only Christianity declares that we are so hopelessly flawed (the biblical term is "sinful") that we can never atone for our sins. It is only by trusting in the work God has performed on our behalf when He sent Christ to die for our sins that we can ever be forgiven by the God whom we have wronged.

How can a person be in a right relationship with God? Every other religion says, "By my own effort and the rules I must keep." Only Christianity says, "By grace." As the apostle Paul wrote, "For by grace you have been saved through faith; and that not of yourselves, it is the gift of God; not as a result of works, so that no one may boast" (Eph. 2:8–9).

The fact that Christianity offers an exclusive, unique answer to humanity's greatest dilemma is one of the strongest arguments for the veracity of the Christian message.

"What about Those Who Have Never Heard of Jesus Christ?"

We devoted an entire chapter (ch. 7) to answering this question in depth, but most people who ask "What about those who have never heard of Jesus Christ?" will not be willing to listen to a lengthy answer. Here are the major talking points to use in answering that question.

Everyone Has Received a Knowledge of God

No one needs to read a Bible or hear a preacher to know there is a God who created this world. One simply needs to look at creation to know that God exists, as Paul declares in Romans 1:20: "For since the creation of the world His invisible attributes, His eternal power and divine nature, have been clearly seen, being understood through what has been made, so that they are without excuse."

God Will Send Additional Knowledge to Those Who Want to Know Him

Simply acknowledging the existence of God is not enough to save a person. However, when someone acknowledges God's

186

existence and sincerely wants to know Him, God will send that person the information he or she needs to know about Jesus Christ. The stories of the conversion of the Ethiopian eunuch (Acts 8:26–40) and the Roman centurion Cornelius (Acts 10) illustrate how God will use whatever supernatural means necessary to send the message of Jesus Christ to those who sincerely want to know Him. It cannot be emphasized too strongly that no one will go to hell for not believing in a Christ of whom they have never heard. Those who spend eternity separated from God will do so for rejecting whatever information about God was available to them.

God Wants to Save As Many People As Possible

The three parables Jesus told in Luke 15 about the lost sheep, the lost coin, and the lost son all reflect God's desire to save, not destroy, those who are alienated from Him. The fact that God would be willing to make the ultimate sacrifice of His own Son for the salvation of the world demonstrates God's love, not His hatred, toward us. As Jesus said, "For God so loved the world, that He gave His only begotten Son, that whoever believes in Him shall not perish, but have eternal life" (John 3:16).

But the fact that God made such a monumental sacrifice for humanity's salvation also underscores the thesis of this book: faith in Jesus Christ alone is the exclusive way for salvation. If alternative paths to heaven are available, why would the Son of God be "delivered over by the predetermined plan and foreknowledge of God" (Acts 2:23) for such a horrendous death? The only logical answer is that faith in Jesus Christ is the exclusive way of salvation for everyone.

"What Happens to Children Who Die before They Are Capable of Believing in Christ?"

There are some truths that unbelievers or new Christians are incapable of comprehending. If you begin talking with an unbeliever about the guilt of children because of the inherited corruption and guilt of the entire human race through Adam (Rom. 5:12), he or she will either stare at you with a befuddled look or will dismiss everything else you say because he or she will assume you are arguing that babies and children go to hell.

In my experience, the best way to answer the question "What happens to children who die before they are capable of believing in Christ?" is to begin with what the questioner wants to hear, because it is what the Bible teaches: babies and children (along with mentally challenged individuals) who are incapable of understanding the gospel of Jesus Christ go to heaven when they die. You can begin with the story of King David's infant son who died, which we reviewed in the last chapter. While his son was ill, David fasted and pleaded for God's healing. But when word came to David that his son had died, David began to eat again and resume his life. The king's servants were perplexed with this sudden change in attitude—especially after hearing that the child had died. David explained, "While the child was still alive, I fasted and wept. . . . But now he has died; why should I fast? Can I bring him back again? I will go to him, but he will not return to me" (2 Sam. 12:22–23). David believed that one day he would join his infant son in the presence of God.

For most people, that assurance is all they need to satisfy the question. However, some who are more theologically astute may persist by asking, "But how can an infant or child be saved without exercising faith in Christ if such faith is required from adults? If infants and children can be saved apart from faith in Christ, why can't adults?"

You can remind the questioner that we are not saved "by faith" but by God's grace, demonstrated by Christ's death for our sins (Eph. 2:8–9). Faith is simply the conduit through which a person receives God's forgiveness into his or her life. The Bible draws a vast distinction between children who are incapable of exercising faith and adult unbelievers who have consciously rejected whatever knowledge about God they have received.

The child or infant who dies before he or she is capable of demonstrating faith is saved the same way as an adult who is capable of demonstrating faith: by the sacrificial death of Jesus Christ. However, God draws a distinction between the child who is incapable of exercising faith and an unbelieving adult who has willfully rejected God's truth.

"How Could So Many People Be Wrong in Their Religious Beliefs?"

Of the seven billion people who reside on planet Earth, only 25 percent could in the broadest sense of the word be classified as "Christian" (and the percentage who have personally trusted in Christ for salvation is much smaller),[4] meaning that over five billion people in the world are destined for hell if indeed Christ offers the exclusive path of salvation. To many, such a conclusion is not only horrific but also irrational. Why?

Many people have been conditioned to accept the oft-quoted maxim "The majority is usually right" and the resulting corollary "The minority is usually wrong." However, Jesus taught that when it comes to the issue of eternal salvation, the opposite is true. The majority of humanity will make the *wrong* choice about the right path to heaven, while the minority of people will chose the right path.

For those who object to the exclusivity of Christ with the "How could so many be so wrong in their religious beliefs?" argument, you can cite Jesus's words in Matthew 7:13–14:

> Enter through the narrow gate; for the gate is wide and the way is broad that leads to destruction, and there are many who enter through it. For the gate is small and the way is narrow that leads to life, and there are few who find it.

If all or the majority of humanity end up in heaven, then Jesus made a mistake in this pronouncement. And if Jesus was wrong about this, then one could assume He may have been wrong about a number of other issues about which He spoke.

However, if the population of heaven will indeed be small compared to the population of hell—a logical assumption that the doctrine of exclusivity leads to—this disturbing disparity between the number of occupants in heaven and hell only confirms the truth of Jesus's words.

"How Could a Loving God Send People to Hell Just for Not Believing the Right Things about Jesus?"

When you encounter this frequent objection to the doctrine of exclusivity, there are two important truths you should highlight, one about God and one about unbelievers.

First, when answering the question "How could a loving God send people to hell just for not believing the right things about

Jesus?" mention that love is one of God's attributes (or you might use the word *characteristics*), but it is not His *only* attribute. For example, if you cared to know something about me, you might ask various people, "What is Robert Jeffress like?" If you asked my wife and daughters, they would probably say, "He's so funny!" If you asked leaders I work with, they might say, "He's intense." If you polled my critics (of which there are many), they might respond, "Jeffress is intolerant." So which is the correct response? Am I funny, intense, or intolerant? In fact, all three are accurate descriptions of me. If I were funny all the time, you would assume I was a clown. Although I'm intolerant of some things, if I were intolerant of everyone and everything, you would assume I was painfully boorish.

What is true of you and me is also true of God. No single characteristic defines the totality of God. The word *love* certainly describes God. The apostle John wrote that "God is love" (1 John 4:8). But notice that John did not claim that "God is *only* love." The Bible also reveals that God is holy (meaning separate and apart from anything or anyone in the universe) and righteous (free from sin). The prophet Habakkuk declared that God's "eyes are too pure to approve evil, and [He] can not look on wickedness with favor" (Hab. 1:13).

God's love means that our Creator desires to have a relationship with us. God's righteousness prevents Him from having fellowship with us and, instead, demands the outpouring of His anger against us. The late theologian Carl Henry wrote, "The modern misjudgment of God flows easily from contemporary theology's preoccupation with love as the core of God's being, while righteousness is subordinated and denied equal ultimacy with love in the nature of the deity."[5]

The cross of Jesus Christ represents the intersection of God's love and God's righteousness. The willingness of God to sacrifice His Son to reconcile us to Himself is a demonstration of His love for us. "But God demonstrates His own love toward us, in that while we were yet sinners, Christ died for us," Paul wrote in Romans 5:8.

But the cross also represents God's righteousness, which demands a payment for our sins. While declaring spiritual amnesty for all people without the cross might be a loving thing for God to do, it would not be a righteous thing for God to do. Someone has to pay for our sin, and the cross is the place where Someone did. As Paul wrote, "Much more then, having now been justified by His blood, we shall be saved from the wrath of God through Him" (v. 9).

Second, the question "How could a loving God send people to hell just for not believing the right things about Jesus?" is built not only on a mischaracterization of God but also on a misunderstanding of the seriousness of unbelief. "Not believing the right things about Jesus" is not nearly as harmless of an offense against God as you might believe.

The unbeliever who has rejected or simply neglected God's offer of salvation through Christ has first of all callously dismissed God's desire for a relationship. The young man who finally summons the courage to tell his girlfriend that he can't live without her and wants to spend the rest of his life with her only to have her say, "I don't think so," or "Let me get back to you on that," understands something of the pain of rejection God feels when we reject His offer of reconciliation with us.

But the unbeliever who rejects the gospel is also guilty of devaluing the sacrifice God has made on our behalf. I think of the media mogul Ted Turner, who reportedly said, "I don't need anybody to die for me. I've had a few drinks and a few girlfriends, and if that's gonna put me in hell, then so be it."

While most unbelievers would not be so bold (or foolish) to voice that sentiment, people who reject God's offer of salvation through Christ are demonstrating the same lack of reverence for the death of God's Son. The author of Hebrews warns:

> How much severer punishment do you think he will deserve who has trampled under foot the Son of God, and has regarded as unclean the blood of the covenant by which he was sanctified, and has insulted the Spirit of grace? (10:29)

The person who refuses to trust in Christ alone for the forgiveness of sins has "trampled under foot the Son of God" (the phrase means to treat as worthless), has declared Christ's blood to be "unclean" (a word referring to the mongrel dogs that roamed Jerusalem), and has "insulted" the Holy Spirit of God, who continually pleads with him or her to trust in Christ. "Not believing the right things about Jesus" is not some minor offense but is tantamount to rejecting God and declaring the death of His Son to be worthless.

Remember, as we said at the beginning of this book, when discussing these seven most common objections to the doctrine of the exclusivity of Christ, our goal is not to win an argument. Instead, always and foremost, our goal is to do the most loving thing we can do for any person—to win him or her to saving faith in God's only way to eternal life: through Christ alone.

Notes

Chapter 1 Christianity's Most Offensive Belief

1. "Dr. Jeffress Discusses Islamic Terrorism on the O'Reilly Factor (10/22/14)," YouTube video, 5:10 (beginning at 3:04), posted by First Baptist Dallas on October 24, 2014, https://www.youtube.com/watch?v=Uyki1qMzfeo.

2. "Viewers Sound Off," *The O'Reilly Factor*, Fox News, October 23, 2014.

Chapter 2 Moving the Fence

1. Justin McCarthy, "Same-Sex Marriage Support Reaches New High at 55%," Gallup, May 21, 2014, http://www.gallup.com/poll/169640/sex-marriage-support-reaches-new-high.aspx.

2. Amy Stern, ed., "A Post-Election Look at Religious Voters in the 2008 Election (Transcript)," *Pew Forum*, December 8, 2008, http://www.pewforum.org/2008/12/08/a-post-election-look-at-religious-voters-in-the-2008-election/.

3. Soumya Karlamangla, "Cardinal Dolan Says Catholic Church 'Caricatured as Anti-gay,'" *LA Times*, November 30, 2013, http://www.latimes.com/nation/nationnow/la-na-nn-cardinal-dolan-gay-marriage-20131130-story.html.

4. "Bill O'Reilly: Gay Marriage Foes Can Only 'Thump the Bible' in Their Arguments (VIDEO)," *Huffington Post*, March 27, 2013, http://www.huffingtonpost.com/2013/03/27/bill-oreilly-gay-marriage-thump-bible_n_2962110.html.

5. Paul Brandeis Raushenbush, "Tim Tebow Officially Puts Evangelical Right on the Sideline," *Huffington Post*, February 21, 2013, http://www.huffingtonpost.com/paul-raushenbush/tim-tebow-first-baptist-dallas_b_2734677.html.

6. The Pew Forum on Religion and Public Life, "Summary of Key Findings," *U.S. Religious Landscape Survey* (February 2008), http://www.pewforum.org/files/2013/05/report-religious-landscape-study-full.pdf.

7. Ibid.

8. "Interview with Joel Osteen," *Larry King Live*, aired June 20, 2005, http://transcripts .cnn.com/TRANSCRIPTS/0506/20/lkl.01.html.

9. D. Martyn Lloyd-Jones, *The Christian Warfare* (Grand Rapids: Baker, 1977), 41–42.

10. Tim Adler, "MIPCOM: Disney-ABC TV Boss Anne Sweeney Says Television Will Get Even More Personal," *Deadline*, October 5, 2011, http://deadline.com/2011/10 /mipcom-disney-abc-tv-boss-anne-sweeney-says-television-will-get-even-more-personal -179592/.

11. David Hinckley, "Average American Watches 5 Hours of TV Per Day, Report Shows," *New York Daily News*, March 5, 2014, http://www.nydailynews.com/life-style /average-american-watches-5-hours-tv-day-article-1.1711954.

12. United States Census, "U.S. and World Population Clock," July 4, 2014, http:// www.census.gov/popclock/.

13. LaTonya Taylor, "The Church of O," *Christianity Today*, April 1, 2002, http://www .christianitytoday.com/ct/2002/april1/1.38.html?start=8.

Chapter 3 Does It Really Matter?

1. John Piper, *Jesus: The Only Way to God—Must You Hear the Gospel to Be Saved?* (Grand Rapids: Baker, 2010), 9.

2. Ronald H. Nash, *Is Jesus the Only Savior?* (Grand Rapids: Zondervan, 1994), 9.

3. "What Americans Believe About Universalism and Pluralism," The Barna Group, April 18, 2011, https://www.barna.org/barna-update/faith-spirituality/484-what-ameri cans-believe-about-universalism-and-pluralism#.VS_XXrpN3zI.

4. Ibid.

5. The Pew Forum on Religion and Public Life, "Summary of Key Findings," *U.S. Religious Landscape Survey* (February 2008), http://www.pewforum.org/files/2013/05 /report-religious-landscape-study-full.pdf.

6. C. S. Lewis, *Letters of C. S. Lewis* (New York: Harcourt, 1966), 428.

7. Rob Bell, *Love Wins* (New York: HarperOne, 2011), 173, 175.

8. Ibid., 108.

9. Rick Rood, "Do All Roads Lead to God? The Christian Attitude toward Non-Christian Religions," *Probe Ministries*, August 30, 1999, https://www.probe.org/do-all-roads-lead -to-god-the-christian-attitude-toward-non-christian-religions/.

10. Piper, *Jesus: The Only Way to God*, 27.

11. Barna Research, as quoted in Robert Jeffress, *Outrageous Truth* (Colorado Springs: WaterBrook, 2008), 5.

12. Lydia Saad, "Three in Four in U.S. Still See the Bible as Word of God," *Gallup*, July 4, 2014, http://www.gallup.com/poll/170834/three-four-bible-word-god.aspx.

Chapter 4 The Old Way Was One Way

1. A. W. Tozer, *The Knowledge of the Holy* (New York: HarperCollins, 2009), 1.

2. I cite much of this evidence in my book *How Can I Know?* (Nashville: Worthy, 2013).

3. J. I. Packer, *Knowing God*, 20th anniversary ed. (Downers Grove, IL: InterVarsity, 1993), 76.

4. Richard Dawkins, *The God Delusion* (New York: Houghton Mifflin Harcourt, 2006), 51.

5. Mark Buchanan, *The Holy Wild* (New York: Crown, 2009), 146.

6. John Ortberg, *God Is Closer Than You Think* (Grand Rapids: Zondervan, 2005), 37–38.

7. G. K. Chesterton, *Orthodoxy* (Chicago: Moody, 2009), 8.

8. Malcolm Muggeridge, as quoted in Philip Yancey, *Rumors of Another World* (Grand Rapids: Zondervan, 2009), 123.

9. Account adapted from Jerome Greer Chandler, *Fire and Rain: A Tragedy in American Aviation* (Austin: Texas Monthly Press, 1986).

Chapter 5 The Intolerant Christ

1. Dorothy Sayers, *Letters to a Diminished Church* (Nashville: Thomas Nelson, 2004), 4, 55.

2. Stephen Flick, "The Christian Origin of the Red Cross," *Christian Heritage Fellowship*, accessed June 4, 2015, http://christianheritagefellowship.com/the-christian-origin-of-the-red-cross/.

3. "About The Salvation Army," The Salvation Army, accessed June 4, 2015, http://salvationarmyusa.org/usn/about.

4. "The Philanthropy 400," *The Chronicle of Philanthropy*, October 30, 2008, 10.

5. John Ortberg, *Who Is This Man?* (Grand Rapids: Zondervan, 2012), 67.

6. Michael Grant, *Jesus: A Historian's Review of the Gospels* (New York: Scribner, 1977), 1.

7. William Beausay II, *Boys! Shaping Ordinary Boys into Extraordinary Men* (Nashville: Thomas Nelson, 1994), 23.

8. "Global Christianity—A Report on the Size and Distribution of the World's Christian Population," Pew Research Center, December 19, 2011, http://www.pewforum.org/2011/12/19/global-christianity-exec/.

9. Clark H. Pinnock, "The Destruction of the Finally Impenitent," *Criswell Theological Review* 4, no. 2 (1990): 246–47, http://www.onthewing.org/user/Esc_Annihilationism%20-%20Pinnock.pdf.

10. Dorothy Sayers, *A Matter of Eternity* (Grand Rapids: Eerdmans, 1973), 86.

11. Charles Stanley, *Eternal Security* (Nashville: Thomas Nelson, 2002), 78–79.

Chapter 6 Why New Testament Jews Were for Jesus

1. Adapted from Erwin W. Lutzer, *Ten Lies about God* (Nashville: Thomas Nelson, 2000), 115.

2. Pope John Paul II, "All Are Called to Build God's Kingdom," general audience address in St. Peter's Square, December 6, 2000, http://w2.vatican.va/content/john-paul-ii/en/audiences/2000/documents/hf_jp-ii_aud_20001206.html.

3. Richard Rohr, *Eager to Love* (Cincinnati: Franciscan Media, 2014), 266.

4. Henri Nouwen, *Sabbatical Journey* (New York: Crossroad, 1998), 51.

5. Dr. Robert H. Schuller, as quoted in Lance Goodall, "Crystal Chaos: The Cathedral's Spiral of Debt," *Christian Witness Ministries*, September 14, 2013, http://www.cwm.org.au/3/18-54/119-4.

6. "The 25 Most Influential Evangelicals in America," *Time*, February 7, 2005, http://content.time.com/time/specials/packages/article/0,28804,1993235_1993243_1993300,00.html.

7. Brian McLaren, "The Sweet Problem of Inclusiveness," *An Emergent Manifesto of Hope*, Doug Pagitt and Tony Jones, eds. (Grand Rapids: Baker, 2008), 194–95.

8. Dallas Willard, "Apologetics in Action," *Cutting Edge*, Winter 2001.

9. *Real Time with Bill Maher*, episode 228, October 14, 2011, http://www.hbo.com /real-time-with-bill-maher/episodes/0/228-episode#/.

10. David Gibson, "Is Pope Francis Endorsing Universalism?," *Charisma News*, May 28, 2013, http://www.charismanews.com/world/39644-is-pope-francis-endorsing-uni versalism.

11. George Barna, *Third Millennium Teens: Research on the Minds, Hearts and Souls of America's Teenagers* (Ventura, CA: Barna Research Group, 1999), 48.

12. Peter Kreeft, *Ecumenical Jihad: Ecumenism and the Culture War* (San Francisco: Ignatius Press, 1996), 156.

13. John Bisagno, as quoted in John Maxwell, *Today Matters* (Nashville: Center Street, 2004), 205.

Chapter 7 What about Those Who Have Never Heard?

1. Bob Smietana, "'In Christ Alone' Dropped from Presbyterian Church Hymnal over Lyric Dispute and Scriptural Debate," *USA Today*, August 7, 2013, reprinted in *Huffington Post*, August 17, 2013, http://www.huffingtonpost.com/2013/08/07/in-christ-alone -dropped_n_3719253.html.

2. Arthur W. Pink, *The Attributes of God* (Grand Rapids: Baker, 1975), 82.

3. Leon Morris, *The Apostolic Preaching of the Cross* (Grand Rapids: Eerdmans, 1968), 35.

4. Charles Spurgeon, "Heaven and Hell: A Sermon," September 4, 1855, *The Spurgeon Archive*, http://www.spurgeon.org/sermons/0039.htm.

5. UCLA Division of Astronomy and Astrophysics, "Frequently Asked Questions in Cosmology," accessed June 4, 2015, http://www.astro.ucla.edu/~wright/cosmology_faq .html#DN.

6. Abubaker Zahoor, "The Size of Milky Way Is 150,000 Light Years, a New Study Challenges the Previous Findings," *TechFrag*, March 16, 2015, http://techfrag.com/2015 /03/16/size-milky-way-150000-light-years-new-study-challenges-previous-findings/.

7. Richard Lewontin, "Billions and Billions of Demons," *The New York Review of Books*, January 9, 1997, http://www.nybooks.com/articles/archives/1997/jan/09/billions -and-billions-of-demons/.

8. Tozer, *Knowledge of the Holy*, 4.

9. Adapted from Charles C. Ryrie, "The Revelation of God," in *Basic Theology: A Popular Systematic Guide to Understanding Biblical Truth* (Chicago: Moody, 1999), chapter 5.

Chapter 8 What about Those Who Could Never Believe in Christ?

1. John F. MacArthur, *Safe in the Arms of God* (Nashville: Thomas Nelson, 2003), 59–60.

Chapter 9 Simple Answers to Complex Questions

1. Robert Jeffress, *Outrageous Truth* (Colorado Springs: WaterBrook, 2008).

2. Khalid Yahya Blankinship, "Sword Verses," *The Oxford Encyclopedia of the Islamic World*, January 2009, http://oxfordindex.oup.com/view/10.1093/acref/978019530 5135.013.0979.

3. Henry Kamen, *The Spanish Inquisition*, 4th ed. (New Haven, CT: Yale University Press, 2014), 253.

4. "Global Christianity—A Report on the Size and Distribution of the World's Christian Population," *Pew Research Center*, December 19, 2011, http://www.pewforum.org/2011/12/19/global-christianity-exec/.

5. Carl F. H. Henry, *Through No Fault of Their Own?*, William V. Crockett and James G. Sigountos, eds. (Grand Rapids: Baker, 1991), 254.

About the Author

Dr. Robert Jeffress is senior pastor of the twelve-thousand-member First Baptist Church, Dallas, Texas, and a Fox News contributor. He is also an adjunct professor at Dallas Theological Seminary. Dr. Jeffress has made more than 1,500 guest appearances on various radio and television programs and regularly appears on major mainstream media outlets such as Fox News Channel's *Fox and Friends*, *The O'Reilly Factor*, and *Cavuto on Business*; ABC's *Good Morning America*; CBS's *This Morning*; HBO's *Real Time with Bill Maher*; CNN's *Anderson Cooper 360*; and MSNBC's *Hardball with Chris Matthews*. Dr. Jeffress hosts a daily radio program, "Pathway to Victory," that is heard nationwide on over eight hundred stations in major markets such as Dallas–Fort Worth, New York City, Chicago, Los Angeles, Washington DC, Houston, and Seattle. His weekly television program can be seen in 195 countries and on 11,283 cable and satellite systems throughout the world, including China and on the Trinity Broadcasting Network and Daystar.

Dr. Jeffress is the author of twenty-one books including *When Forgiveness Doesn't Make Sense, Perfect Ending: Why Your Eternal Future Matters Today,* and his newest book, released on February 10, *Countdown to the Apocalypse: Why ISIS and Ebola Are Only the Beginning.* Dr. Jeffress recently led his congregation in the completion of a $135 million re-creation of its downtown campus. The project is the largest in modern church history and serves as a "spiritual oasis" covering six blocks of downtown Dallas.

Dr. Jeffress has a DMin from Southwestern Theological Seminary, a ThM from Dallas Theological Seminary, and a BS from Baylor University. In May 2010 he was awarded a Doctor of Divinity degree from Dallas Baptist University, and in June 2011 he received the Distinguished Alumnus of the Year award from Southwestern Baptist Theological Seminary.

Dr. Jeffress and his wife, Amy, have two daughters, Julia and Dorothy, and a son-in-law, Ryan Sadler.

NOT ALL ROADS LEAD TO HEAVEN

Complete DVD Teaching Set

Teaching set includes...

» A hard-cover copy of NOT ALL ROADS LEAD TO HEAVEN

» The complete, unedited nine-message series on DVD

» A CD-ROM with printer-friendly message notes and study questions for Sunday school classes and small groups

» A comprehensive instructor's guidebook, complete with answers to study questions and expanded responses to key points

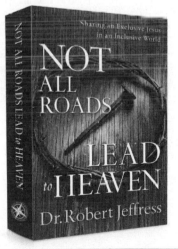